CHAINS BROKEN

By Flora Samuel

Copyright © 2012 Flora Samuel

All rights reserved.

ISBN-13:978-0615674001

Chains Broken

Matters of the Heart
On Being Delivered

By Flora Samuel

TABLE OF CONTENTS

Page 1	Matters of the Heart, on Being Delivered
Page 2	The Pilgrimage to Deliverance
Page 2	Experiences
Page 7	The experience God used & My Story
Page 11	Re-dedication of my life to Christ
Page 12	The Heartbreak & Journey Continued
Page 15	Change took place & The Pilgrimage
Page 20	Lesson Learned
Page 23	The Choice-to see the bigger picture
Page 24	Sobriety VS Intoxication
Page 25	Changed behavior by transformed thinking
Page 30	The oppressed mind
Page 34	The offense & more experiences & revelations
Page 42	Where do I go from here
Page 46	The key
Page 54	Funeral services (For bad thoughts)
Page 57	DNR placed
Page 55	Life continues
Page 64	Freedom & victory found in Christ only
Page 77	The Salvation Question
Page 78	The invitation
Page 81-82	Spiritual blessings & affirmations
Page 84-85	Testimonies of God's grace
Page 86	Thoughts from the author
Page 87	Words from the author
Page 88	Prayers

Dedication

This book is dedicated to the Body of Christ; it is my prayer and desire that we become "HONEST" with ourselves. Then and only then can we become free to experience the freedom that was so dearly paid for us by our Lord on the cross of Calvary; an incredible purchased price; His life….

Becoming honest will open the flood gates of heaven for a new level of living, one that is full of joy. This is the original purpose and intent of our Father. His plan for our lives have not changed. He said I knew you before you were formed in your mother's womb. Jeremiah 1:5, in addition, you were predestined (predetermined-before hand) before the foundations of the world that you would be conformed to the image of Christ, God's Son, and the likeness of your Father. Romans 8:29-30-your predetermined existence and destiny to be conformed to the image of Christ; so you can't help but become all that God planned for you… Amen

We are to rule and reign like the Father in heaven and use the authority in the earth like Jesus did during His earthly ministry.

We came out of the "Godhead" by a spoken word, Genesis 1:26A let "Us" make man in our image and our likeness; then at a time specified you were born (your natural birth into the earth realm) by Him to be a living witness of His glory and His goodness. He said His Word will not return to Him empty-void; it will accomplish full everything it is intended to accomplish. See Isaiah 55:11

ON BEING DELIVERED, HEALED AND SET-FREE

My Journey of Deliverance

My Power of Choice

My Testimony

MY STORY AS REAL AS ITS GETS

Chronologically Told
Experiences took place over many years

(Some things are written in the past tense and some are in the present tense, depending on how I wrote them as the Holy Spirit revealed them during the deliverance)

Acknowledgements

I would like to thank my dear friends Suzanne Wells and Latrell Carr, without both of whom, it would have been almost impossible to complete the work. I would like to thank my husband Sidney for allowing the quiet time needed to complete the work and for all the days my pancakes and cups of coffee were served to me at the computer. Thanks also honey for all the nice cold glasses of water served to me by you. I love you. I would like to thank my daughter Latricia for believing she has the best mom in the whole world and my son Tyrone for encouraging me all the way to do the work. I want to thank all who said "Yes", "Yes", do it.

MATTERS OF THE HEART, ON BEING DELIVERED

Most of us who need deliverance need healing also; healing from wounds and pains that have caused us to shut down and to shrink back. Healing is also needed in areas of disappointments, perceived failures, relationships gone bad, for those things that didn't work out the way we wanted them to, missed opportunities and jobs, bad bosses, pastors and leaders who were not after God's heart.

Most of all the body of Christ is dealing with generational up-bringing, mental and emotional handicaps, challenges and difficulties; just plain ole wrong thinking. Your life now is because of your yesterdays, your childhood and the way you were brought up. I found that my challenges started and were from my childhood, then later in life my battle became my own mind. I had to fight the way and manner in which I perceived life and its events, circumstances and situations.

Dealing with a troubled mind, a battle to the death of one or the other.

A battle to the death of one mind set over the other; either bondage or freedom; dealing with mindsets that are contrary to the will of God for my life, your life and what is best for our lives. It is a battle to the death, a day to day combat, a place where no one can tell you that life can be different or any other way than the way you are experiencing it and have experienced in the past. The voices of bad experiences, situations and circumstances are screaming louder than the voice of faith; (Faith in God).

A journey-my life as it was before deliverance & The pilgrimage to deliverance

The un-shackling of my mind-the breaking of chains, the way I thought

I didn't even believe that it was possible to think another way, or that there is even another way of thinking, I didn't even believe that it is meant for me to be another way than the way I was. (The experience that I was experiencing at the time), I didn't believe (because of doubt) that I was supposed to have a different life, one that is full of love, joy and happiness. My life circumstances were trying to convince me that I was in bondage to this thing for life, "FOREVER", I thought there was no way out, no way I could be free.

My experiences voices were louder and more convincing then at that time; because they didn't have any oppositional teaching or alternate experiences to oppose the bondage mindset. I can truly say it has been my own mind that I have had to battle these last 17 years; a new way of thinking challenging the old. See you can't even fathom, dream or think there is an alternative, another way of living and being than the experience you are in middle of.

You see, I too have been in the "Ring" the battle ring-the fight to the death of one or the other and it seemed as though I would never win the fight over mindset, it seemed as though it would prevail.

Experiences

I am going to share this until the end, until we all get it. I know you think you have it already but you don't because if you were already free, we would be living a different life, one that is full of love and joy, one that will not cause us to feel bad day after day, doubting ourselves every step of the way.

It is my heart's cry that connects me to my Lord; He died for us to have this life, what a price was paid, His life and you tell me that we are not meant to have this joyous life? The devil is a liar.

My experiences lied to me. Or was it the way I saw, viewed and perceived them that haunted, tormented and discouraged me? Was experience my enemy? Or was it my viewpoint and mindset of them, which was the enemy. Either way I was battling with a real determined destroyer.

My entire battle was my own mind, being influenced too much, by Satan through things that could be seen or viewed by my natural senses. My circumstances were being touched satanically with the purpose of convincing me that any true level of freedom and spirituality in God was "UNATTAINABLE". To make matters worse it caused me to occasionally go into sin, the time had been so long, "years", I would become worn out-weary in well-doing, and tired of fighting especially when I knew I wanted to do what was right and pleasing to the Lord; yet I couldn't. This would wake up a whole other subject, the demon of already feeling like I didn't measure up. Here was just one more thing I couldn't do right or get right, a "perfect" faith-filled relationship with God.

I needed to do it better, to do it just right. I needed to do it like other people. See, they were doing it right, what was wrong with me? This threw me heavily into "WORKS", the works of the flesh, which caused even further damage, it set me up for failure, the very thing I tried so hard not to do. It made me feel worse.

Others got it right and God blessed them. What is wrong with me? Then the false accusing of God would come in, doubt of God's intentions for me and my life. The good He had called me to and the good for my life.

So before I go too far on this "experience" let me get back to where I was the unattainable view I had of God. I can remember one time I said to myself (as though it was a secret from God) that

I might as well do this or do that, but usually it was fornication, a sexually based relationship (looking for love in all the wrong places) all I ever wanted and desired was love, I must tell you it was usually with men so unworthy of the costly decision I was making at the time, they had no idea or comprehension of the value I was giving away for cheap.

Usually they were men who themselves had emotional problems and they normally got their egos fed through wanton and extremely needy women like I once was. The defilement of my temple was now the open door for Satan to come in and emotionally bind me with oh much emotional baggage that comes from a trespass as such and from an un-renewed mind. Un-renewed by the Word of God, now, not meaning that it's just going to zap your mind and everything would be ok again; I needed to spend un-imaginable amount of time and hours in the presence of the Lord through His Word to receive healing and deliverance.

The effects of a viewpoint of an unattainable goal, was one of discouragement, the old what is the use thoughts and words would be whispered, it will never happen, I will never get it, I will never reach it. Discouragement forever was on the journey with me. Then it would be joined by its relative, "self-pity", which was a lack of faith. I wasn't there yet-walking in unshakeable faith, so I was perishing by my every thought from the lack of knowledge and understanding of the knowledge and revelation that I was already more than a conqueror through Him who loves me, believing what God has said about me in His Word.

Being able to endure the long awaited joy that everyone speaks of including God; when it looks and appears that everybody else is doing fine, they are doing great; it's just you that is not. I begin to realize though that I was too focused on me-(self), I realized how much was centered on "ME" and that definitely was a problem. It was constantly what I feel, what I see, what I am experiencing, and even though our feeling and emotions are a real part of our lives, we must not allow them to control us, we should not be govern by them, especially when they are of the old nature, their origins are of the Adamic nature.

Self-pity, it says and it always ask, why is it happening to me and why is it taking so long for me to be blessed? You see, I was identifying too much with me, what I can feel, what I was feeling and not enough on the promises of God. Doing this allowed offense and anger at God and others to enter in.

What do you do when what you are doing is destroying you, when you don't know anything else at the time? You can't relate to anything else because this is all you know and all you've ever experienced. This is all you can relate to, it is your only reference and your whole existence and being are centered on (your perceived) failures, unfair and unhappy experiences, you know nothing else and the enemy and your mind only remind you of your preconceived failures and shortcomings and it would come when I was already feeling down and beating myself up, it was when I couldn't derive anything different than what I was "FEELING", "EXPERIENCING" and this enforced the preconceived failure mindset, which in turn caused depression and discouragement like no other life experience could.

Discouragement, at this time I had no other frame of reference to draw from, I had been beaten down by life at this point, oh there is and had always been the Word of God, but how could I believe that at the point I was at, my life experiences were screaming the lie, the loudest at the time, they had the biggest mouth and were getting all the attention. My life had been one perceived defeated experience after the other. This was looming so large that I couldn't see anything else at this time and I would have called you a liar if you tried to tell me something different than what I believed and was also experiencing.

Understand that I was not living if I was not combating two mindsets, one of bondage and one of desire for freedom. Life had no purpose and no meaning. What was the use or the reason for living if I was not in combat (internally) with the two mindsets? I gauged my life by the intensity of the battle. This would feed my need to have self-pity. I needed to have a reason for being and feeling miserable. By now it's my very existence. I knew no other except misery and she was the company I kept; being inferior to everything and everybody. This was where I got my identity from.

You are asking me to be something and someone that I know nothing of or about, you say just believe God, just have faith, just this and just that, now I am angry, because I don't think you understand me or my pain, (see I even had ownership of the pain), what I am going through, poor me, (self-pity). I need you to feel sorry for me too, like I was doing and feeling, don't you see it, I need this desperately, you are blowing my high, I need this fix, self-pity and I am angry with you if you don't know it and won't give it to me.

You see this was my only way of living, surviving and if you didn't become a partaker in it and enable me, I'd see you as my enemy. I didn't want anything to do with you (the work of the enemy), if I viewed you as the enemy I would not trust you and therefore would not receive anything from you, like the serious deliverance that I needed at the time. I would not receive a word of encouragement from you. My identity had begun to come from the negative only at this point. I had a malignant growth of wrong thinking, if I also perceived you to be successful, you would serve only as a reminder that I was not what I was supposed to be, desired to be or not as good as you.

Again a battle to the death one mind set over the other of freedom; it is a battle to the death, one has to die, has to go. It is a day to day combat. No one can tell you that life can be different than the one I was experiencing and had experienced before.

My Story, in 1987 I married a man that I did not know very long. I met him through a dating service. I'm going to give you just a quick and short blurb of what took place before 1990. I was 34 years of age and innocent or should I say naïve to life and what it was all about. I married this man, from a different culture.

This was the experience that God would use to bring about His purpose for my life..

I married him very quickly, I asked him if he wanted to get married and he said yes. We began to spend time away from each other, (employment purposes); he took a job in another city and that in and of itself became the catalyst for problems. (Unbridled by the Holy Spirit), then I joined him in Orlando, Florida. We were there for approximately a year or so then things became really strained. I sought counseling, I hated to go home and he said he hated for me to come home.
Things became so bad until I would leave the house when he came home and would sit in my car across the street in a Publix supermarket and Eckerd parking lot until I thought he was asleep for the night around eleven pm. Things ended up with me moving back home for about ten months. I submerged myself in church and he would come home on the weekends. I finally convinced him to go to a counseling session with me and the pastor was forthright and truthful, he told him and me if he did not work on the marriage it would not last.

Against all odds and better judgment I relocated with him again to a different city, Melbourne, Florida. I landed a job at the local mall as a cosmetic consultant. By this time my husband had found extracurricular activities; ones that definitely add to the deterioration of any relationship, another woman, but my pain and torture were the mental and emotional abuse. He would withdraw himself; he would not want to participate in the marital duties of a partner. I would beg to be close to him and he would not give in. The marriage became so lonely that at times I would get into my car and go down a dark road and just cry until I thought I would lose my mind. I would sit and wait for God to come as I would do often and sit in the car with me in the natural, (talking about crazy with pain) because I knew that if He didn't I was not going to make it.

Things got so bad until we began to have physical fights, tear and break down everything in the house. My teenage son, in high school at the time was witnessing all of this. There were times my husband would try to leave and I would block the door so that he could not leave. Eventually, he would shove me out of the way and leave anyway. Eventually also we became like total strangers, totally separate, like roommates instead of husband and wife living in the same house and household items such as food, right down to the toothpaste were duplicated, because he had his and I had mine; the insanity went on for some time.

Then one night (remember all this is happening and I am saved), we had a big fight because one evening when I came home he had washed out his underwear and shirt, as though he had been up to something, that pushed me over the edge, with everything else I was dealing with, a cheating husband. One of his women had come to the house and pretended that she wanted to buy a car we had for sale. He was so nervous that he got rid of her in a hurry.

During this time between Orlando and Melbourne we had taken a trip also to Europe to visit his children and during our visit there he stayed out all night. I was horrified, we had an argument, got past that and returned home, however, remnants or should I say the after effects of his staying out all night on our trip began to show up, pictures of women and their times. He had gotten a Post Office Box to receive the letters and the communications. I left him again. But now back to Melbourne, where we continued to be married until the night of the big fight I mentioned earlier. That night I must have had enough of all the fights and rejections. I decided that night I was going to go to bed and have a good night's rest. This was after he had stormed out of the house and I realized this time I did not even try to stop him. I did go to bed and next day I went to work.
I asked this girl I had met if she knew of any place or anybody that I could stay with for a while. It just so happened that she lived in a three-bedroom house with one other roommate and a third roommate was needed to help with the expenses. That day I

accepted it, went home and got all my things, actually only my clothes. I left a house full of furniture and dishes. I just needed peace of mind in my soul. As I was leaving with the last load of my things I saw him coming home. Thank God I missed him.

Weeks passed and one day I went over there and while I was there a woman came over also, she soon left because I think it was uncomfortable for her. Then again I went over and we were intimate, (thought I could save the marriage), I believe I spent the night. The next day was Saturday and he said he had to go to Orlando; he would phone me when he returned. Then the day came when he should have returned, but no call came, it began to be late in the evening still no call, night came, no call. Sunday came and still no call, I became panic stricken, I left numerous messages, then I called again and he finally answered the phone. He was so nasty and cruel, he told me to never call his number again. This sent me into panic, a rage like never before. I began to shake uncontrollably at work, I had to leave, I was unable to control myself, and the pain I felt. I could not drive so I phoned someone to pick me up. I went over there; I wanted to kill him, to cause him pain like he had caused me.

Then approximately one year later I decided it was time to set myself free emotionally so one day a friend and I went and picked him up on his lunch break from his job and we went to the courthouse. I filed for divorce and I paid for it because all I wanted was to be free. I decided this time to stay in the same city; I said this time I was not going to uproot myself again; I had done it too many time before.

During that year before filing for divorce I buried myself in the Lord and everything about Him. The marriage ended. I would experience the worst loneliness that a person could ever experience. I don't know how all of it came about; it was though it was a nightmare, I was under the spell of it. What had started it all? I experienced loneliness in the first degree; this became a spirit that would haunt me for years to come. I would still get into my car at night and go down a dark road and just cry out to God, knowing that if He didn't come and sit in that car with me, I would not make it; I would not survive. I was so hurt and lonely that I became suicidal. He (now my ex-husband) two husbands back, and that is another story for another time, maybe a 2nd book. Freedom in truth.... He was an emotionless and distant spouse. This was the devastating onset of trials that would follow for years to come, while the revelation and full knowledge of Christ Jesus would be revealed to me and be made known to me. Remember, God was perfecting-working out His plan for my future and destiny in Him.

1990, the year of re-dedication of my life to Christ, Orlando, Florida.

I was brought up in church my entire life, it was here that I re-committed my life to the Lord. I had been baptized early in life and went to church faithfully my entire life, you know it was the traditional thing to do, but it was here that I embarked on a new and different Spiritual Journey that would forever change my life. I gave my heart and life to Jesus. I had known God all my life, but now a personal relationship was birthed, one that would forever be evolving, reaching new heights and eternal glory. Jesus Christ became my Lord and Savior anew and afresh. Little did I know that my life would never be the same again and that ahead of me lie the most challenging of times one could ever experience?

Like Job I would experience what it meant to lose everything and everybody that ever meant anything to me. I want to tell you that God is **"Faithful"**-which is His Essence-His being, this is my message to you. From my heart to yours a triumphal journey that started from heartbreak; a journey I thought certain not to make it through, but God had other plans and to Him be the glory......

We all enter our journeys either through our passions, our struggles or our beliefs; for me it was my beliefs and my struggles.

Sit back and go on the journey with me

Lose yourself, let yourself go and if you find yourself while on the journey with me, keep reading, you will find a new you emerged at the end.

The Heartbreak, at 39 years of age I found myself on what would be for the next decade the most challenging time of my life, a separation ending in divorce; the experience that changed my life, the heartbreak of a life time. The heartbreak at 39 years of age almost proved fatal emotionally. All my illusions about life were burst, my naivety regarding life served as a weapon in this experience. I soon learned that my family and my upbringing had not prepared me properly to handle situations such as a separation from someone whom you love and cherish and couldn't imagine your life without. The following months and years would prove to be the most challenging times of my life.

The Journey, the first year after the divorce I was as a zombie, just existing from day to day with no direction or hope. Who would have known that the next ten years would bring about such a profound change in my life, to the degree that I would never be the same again. The already broken pieces of my heart continued to be broken until there was nothing left it felt like. I immersed myself into my work and new found spirituality. Before the rise, little did I know that the shattering of my spirit would continue before the healing would begin to surface.

In June 1992 with a question to my Creator a foundation was laid a new foundation was poured for my life; one that only He would build upon. The newly structured foundation became a firm and strong building (vessel) never to be shaken again to the degree it had been after the separation. As time progressed, I spent most of my time in dedication to the spiritual journey I had embarked upon. It became my life-line; the source of my survival.

If someone had told me that I would recover from such an emotional upheaval I would have called them a liar. It was at this time that God sent me an angel; a real live one. Her name is Mary Martha; she is from Russia, who would have thought she would be sent on an assignment to a broken-hearted girl in South Florida. She was this beautiful blonde and her contents were one of love. In the next decade, she would become to me what a mother is to an infant; my caregiver, both naturally and spiritually. She was the instrument through which God would resurrect my life. She became the most influential person in my life. I was as an infant, I had to be spoon-fed and carefully, so not to cause me to regurgitate what I had taken in. (the things I had learned about God). I had to learn to live again. This experience was one of death, both emotionally and spiritually. I could only imagine the cost to her for taking on such a responsibility. It had to be a great sacrifice for her, because of the time and energy I would require in the coming weeks and months. It was a great undertaking. Our connection took place after a weekly church service; there she was standing at the rear where I would be exiting. That moment our hearts were knitted together in the Spirit. She found my heart in a state of heaviness, heavy-laden with heart-ache. She took me in her arms and allowed me to cry until there were no tears remaining, at least for that day.

Her beautiful blonde hair and suit was stained with my tears, tears she would forever hold dear; years later she told me that she never had that particular suit dry cleaned; it was too sentimental; after all, those same tears God had bottled up in heaven.

I entered a new threshold, birthed into a new dimension. Approximately twenty to thirty minutes later she looked into my eyes; and asked, Flora, what keeps you from walking through that door that God has opened for you? We then walked outside and she walked with me as a father to be or a nurse would pregnant woman; as to help speed along the labor pains (heart pains) my response to her question was one of pain to give, I cried out "my family", "my family". That day I prayed a relinquishment prayer, to release everything and everybody that was considered a hindrance to me accessing that open door. Releasing everything that would weigh me down from reaching the new heights that were now set before me. I was now to be of Kingdom's use and Kingdom use only.

In June 1992, I asked God a second question after reading a passage in a book given to me called the "Recovering of Psalms" by a friend after my divorce; yes the separation did end in divorce. If you heal broken hearts, why haven't you healed mine? That day something seemed to break, then one day on the way to my hometown, God gave me what I accepted as an answer to my question to Him, He was healing my heart; He gave me the reason for the pain, trials and heartache, He said from this day forth I am to refer to myself as an Evangelist. I would spread the Good News of the Gospel and tell others of my journey.

The divorce was the cruel ending of an era passed in my life. In the Judge's chamber sitting face to face with my soon to be ex-husband, he was erected in pride as he had been in times past. I wondered how all this could have happened. When it was over, on my trip home from the courthouse, I had a gut-wrenched cry, and then turned that page of my life as it had been him and I, and the book was closed.

The Total Woman, who is she; she is whole, spiritually, physically and emotionally. She is me. I now in return as thanks to my triumphant journey give back what was given to me; II Corinthians 1:2-4. I encourage all who are wounded and discouraged in spirit. For those that are wrapped in pretty packages on the outside, but bleeding on the inside, I give them "HOPE".

Flora Samuel

1992 – Change took place

A spiritual awakening took place, how much I have come to depend upon my Lord. How He has drawn me near to Him and fulfilled every need I had and more. He took His finger and wiped away the tears, He healed and anointed with His very own love every hurt and wound I had.
As I became naked and helpless He gave me a robe of righteousness to cover me. As He gently removed the diseased flaws, "(bondage mindsets)", He gently and lovingly inserted parts of Himself to replace and fill the places He had cleaned out; then after the big surgery was done, I was recuperating and from time to time little roots cropped up, but as He saw them and He allowed me to see them too, He would come along ever so gently as not to disturb the work He had already done, He would remove the roots, to never again crop up. The little places where they were He inserted more of His character; more of Himself.

Oh my brothers and sisters, if you could only but for a moment feel the love of God from a once upon a time shattered heart, to one that is full of joy, peace and love. My cup runneth over!!!!

The Pilgrimage to Deliverance continues:

The unshackling of the mind, believing that you're supposed to have a different life than one in bondage, to having one that is full of joy, love and happiness. Our life circumstances convince us that we are in bondage to these things until death. Not yet spiritual enough to do combat with the soulish realm, (Your mind) and in touch too much with the senses, but we have a choice and we can make a decision.

I was being influenced too much, by the enemy (Satan) and my own un-renewed mind in some areas, through my senses, my circumstances and situations. They were all being touched with the purpose of convincing me that any true level of freedom in God was unattainable. Trying to convince me to give up and

become weary in well-doing. During this long period of testing, I would still occasionally go off into sin, I would become worn out and tired of fighting especially when I knew I wanted to do what was right, but yet I couldn't and this would remind me of that old spirit and subject of feeling inadequate, that I didn't measure up, wasn't good enough, I didn't do it just right, I need to do it better like other people do, they get it right and God blesses them. (Walking by sight is deadly to your victorious walk that you can have through faith).
I would ask myself in my mind, (again as though it was a secret from God) what is wrong with me; then the false accusing again of God would come in, doubt of God's intentions for me and my life; the good He had called me to. Before I go any further on this experience let's go back to the reason for all this; it was the unattainable view and thoughts I had of God.

I can remember again, like a few times before, I said to myself that I might as well do this. Usually it was an un-godly relationship. This man like the others was unaware of my value, he too was so unworthy of the costly decision I made to be with him. The defilement of my temple, the now open door for Satan to (legally) come in and again emotionally bind me with all the emotional baggage that comes from ungodly soul-ties and from un-renewed minds; which would require hours and hours in the presence of the Lord, immersed in His Word to receive freedom from this type of bondage.

The effects of a viewpoint of an unattainable goal; it brings discouragement. The old "what's the use" thoughts and ideas came "it will never happen" "demons whispers in your ear" "it'll never happen", you'll never get it" and "you'll never reach it".
Discouragement continued to be a traveler on my journey and then from discouragement its relative "self-pity" which was from a lack of faith still traveled the journey with me. I had not reached mature faith not quite yet. I was perishing still from lack of knowledge and understanding; still not believing what God said about me in His Word in certain areas of my life.

Being able to endure the long awaited joy that everyone speaks of including God, when it looks as if everybody else is doing fine, they are doing ok, it was a great test of faith; my faith. I continued to realize how much was centered on me though, what I felt, what I could see and what I was experiencing. While experiences are a very real part of our lives, they shape our outlook on things, but like our feelings, again we are not to be governed or ruled by them, we can learn from them though. Allowing my feelings and the outlook about my experiences to govern and dictate to me fostered emotional pain. They were my wrong thoughts about the experiences that I was experiencing.

Self-pity asks and says why is this happening to me and why am I not being blessed like others? (Always comparing our growth and success to someone else's). See I was identifying too much of self and comparing it to others, this is where the defeat by Satan comes in, because he will always give your mind a picture of someone you think is doing better than you. (What a setup by the enemy of our souls). Then the offense and anger at God comes. So what do you do when what you are doing is destroying you, when you don't know anything else at the time, you can't relate to anything else because this is all you've ever experienced?
This is all you know, this is all you can think of and about, all you can relate to. Your whole existence is centered and focused around what you thought were unfair and unhappy experiences. How can you separate your experiences from your worth, your true identity? You don't know how and this breeds and feeds discouragement like no other. What else can you relate to?

Oh, but there is another reference, there is the Word of God, but I was in the middle of a battle for my sanity, so who could believe that at this time and space in my life? Right. My experiences were screaming the loudest at that time and they were getting the most attention (my mind stayed on them instead of God), after all what else could I identify with, when with my life it had been perceived one defeat after the other. Notice I said perceived (viewed)- thought of in a specific way-which was the enemy's strategy all along, to convince me that God's promises to me are not "Yea" and "Amen". That my freedom had not been purchased by Jesus on the Cross of Calvary.

The experience was looming large, I could not see anything else at the time and you couldn't convince me if you tried; to tell me something different than what I felt, what I thought and was experiencing. See the experiences were a formidable foe, challenging the Word of God, so they got all the attention; after all I had come to the place where I thought I was not living if I was not combating two mindsets. Life had come to the point of no purpose, no meaning. What's the use for living if I was not in combat (internally) with the two mindsets? I had found reasons for living in the chaos and abuse-turbulent mindsets. Thinking this was all there was to life, this was all I knew and I gauged life by the intensity of the battle. (Ladies you know this drill right). This would feed my need to have self-pity. I had a reason for being and feeling miserable. By now it's my very existence.

I knew no other except misery; she was the company I kept; inferior to everything and everybody. This was where I got my identity from. You are asking me to be something and someone that I know nothing of, nothing about? How to just believe God, just have faith, just this and just that, now I am angry, because I don't think you understand my pain, what I'm going through (poor me)-self-pity, I need for you to feel sorry for me like I am doing, don't you see it? I need this fix of you helping me to have self-pity and I am angry with you if you don't know it, won't give it to me or join me. See this is my only way of living and surviving. If you don't become a partaker (enable me), I see you as my enemy, I didn't want anything to do with you (this was the work of the enemy), see you have deliverance for me or to point me in the way of it, but because I viewed you as the enemy I wouldn't receive from you or take from you because I didn't trust you. I was spiritually sick with a malignant growth of wrong thinking. My identity was coming from a negative point of view of life. This kept me from being responsible for myself, like all who feel it is always someone else's fault for their misery.

If I viewed you as successful, doing the ministry and having the call of God fulfilled in your life, I would find fault with you and everything you did, therefore blocking any kind of positive or possible growth I could receive from you; which was Satan's intent; anything to keep me in bondage and for as long as he could.

July 13, 2001-Another lesson learned
It's a relationship, not life, not God, only He deserves such allegiance. It's a job, not the source, only the channel in which God uses to bless me. Quit giving things and people so much value. That is why I was disappointed, to the point of being depressed over the loss of things and loves. I learned the only reason this happens is because I gave it and them too much value, which in turn gave it too much control in my life. It became large in my life due to my perspective, which was due to the assignment of value I had given. That was why I became so disappointed when they didn't live up to my expectations, to the largeness I had given them. I became so devastated about it only because I had given it so much value more value than it deserved, because it's true worth was nothing in comparison to the value I had given them. I had assigned a worth to it in a major way which was not true worth, only built up in my mind.

Because of their fallible state, both man and things, it best behooves a person never, ever give a thing or a person so much value because it will fail you, will let you down, only God deserves the blessings of my allegiance and thanksgiving in such a major amount. It was built up in my head- my mind, it was not really that large- that worth in its true state, only my idea of it, of him and them. So I gave it unhealthy proportions of my dedication and allegiance, which it (normally a relationship) truly did not deserve.

I had them so high until I had to look up to them therefore in turn placing more value on them, as though I had to live up to their standards, when my standards, my morals were probably already higher than theirs, but I didn't know my own value, so I sold myself short, they needed to measure up to me, not me to them. I had it backwards due to my wrong perspective, wrong view of them and things, but most of all the inadequate view I had of myself. I assigned un-realistic (due to their fallible state) value to them.

I gave them such importance and value until I feared losing them, or it, because I thought I wouldn't be able to make it without this person or this thing in my life. (I had never done the street thing or the drug or alcohol scene, grew up in church; so the only avenue Satan could access and have some level of success with was through a malnourished, under-fed need of love I had and I yearned and would have given anything to have it). A man was Satan's ticket and I might add he used it well on me, until I came into the knowledge of who Christ was and I was in Him. Amen, Amen....

I needed so desperately love and affection, (now you understand the man thing), and because I didn't even know I had a life outside of my emotions. I thought all life existed in my feelings, what I could feel and my emotions. This was a huge success for Satan for a time and times. I would become seriously angry with those who would not return to me in the same proportion and dedication as I was giving and trying to hold onto in strength, it made me crazy with resentment. I felt rejected and I now know it was due to my own inappropriate and unhealthy value I had placed upon the thing or the person, the object of my affection.

I feared losing these things due to the unhealthy attachments I had formed with them and this caused me to stay in the unhealthy relationships even when I knew they were no longer workable, I knew they were bad. Change was hard for me because of fear, so I didn't with open arms receive or adapt to any change readily. Once I had gotten comfortable (when in abuse) and ladies we can adjust ourselves to abuse and live a lie for almost a lifetime if we are not careful and alert. Even when I had the gut feeling (spirit unction) that I should not get involved, even when it was hard to adjust to from the start of the relationship, I still didn't want to make changes, even though change was necessary, fear made me un-assured of myself, I wasn't sure of myself enough to make the adjustments needed, I feared losing control.

I would adjust myself (talking about the sacrifice of your peace, your emotions, and your joy); I would adjust myself to the bad behavior to the emotional torture. I would find a place of tolerance for this un-healthy and bad relationship where I felt in control (normally through losing myself), what a price, but, never-the-less I would feel somewhat in control, not realizing it was a self-destroying control I had found.

I didn't realize that I could be happy if I allowed the function of the Holy Spirit to operate and grow within me, allowing a good relationship to grow at its own pace, I didn't have to control it, there were people, other good men, godly men who wanted to be with me and I didn't have to squeeze the life out of them by holding onto them for dear life to be with me. This is the healthy place of a relationship which I had not reached yet. I failed to recognize that I was worth staying with due to my value and the value I brought to the relationship and the part I brought to make it a whole union.

I realized that I had never given myself the proper props that were due to me. Others were willing to give them to me, but I didn't realize it, because I wasn't giving them to myself. I was not giving myself the credit that was due to me from me, not others, but from me. I have since learned it doesn't matter how someone feels about you, how someone views you, the most important of all is; **"HOW DO YOU SEE YOURSELF"** YOUR SELF-PORTRAIT IS THE MOST IMPORTANT FACTOR ABOUT YOURSELF.....
I needed to properly validate my own self-worth-in my own eyesight. It was no one else; it was me, who was short-changing me. I forgave myself for not giving myself the props that were due to me, and I have now turned to a new page of life itself, in abundance; **I am fearfully and wonderfully made, I was created in the very likeness and image of God, it doesn't get any**

better.. Amen…

I am Woman, God's Handmaiden, I am the Bride of Christ, I am betrothed to one lover, one Husband and His name is Jesus…. Talking about worth and value-There is none greater.. Amen

Choosing to see the bigger picture of my life

Yes, I lived these experiences, God used them and His glory was revealed, so that the power and the ability of God through grace for my life could be witnessed. Who said all this was wrong, four marriages and two husbands, married them each twice. Take the blind man in the bible; was it a good thing to be blind or ask the crippled, or the woman sick for 12 years? No, certainly not, right? These things could only be understood by having spiritual insight, so were and are my experiences. So if my shortcomings, trials and tests were to be used by God for His glory, then I think all these things were a good thing to have experienced. I found comfort in these words of David, **"Many are the afflictions of the righteous; but the Lord delivereth him out of them all". Psalms: 34:19.**

To be worthy to be counted for God's glory as the Apostles said; to be counted worthy to suffer for God's glory, I would say is a good thing. After all, not everybody gets "considered" as Job did or be counted worthy for God to show His hand mightily on their behalf. Amen. To be a witness for Jesus is paramount.

My wounds were alive and extremely painful, but now I get to share them, to be a witness for the delivering power of our Almighty God. To tell, to be a witness for Jesus, how else are people going to get to see and know the power of God? Just by them reading it, by just talking about it, but without the experience of it? I think not…. Go and be a witness.. Amen.

The conclusion of choosing (a deliberate action made) to see the bigger picture of my life as a wonderful and experiential journey, I declared that my life was not a mistake. God gave me His grace to cover me until I came into the knowledge and maturity of His Son Jesus Christ. The experiences are what made it all real to me. See, I was never alone, the Lord was with me all the time and all the way, after all, remember, He promised us that He would never leave or forsake us…..

Sobriety VS Intoxication-Life continues……
I recall looking back, I had two kinds of days, some were sober ones and others were heavily intoxicated with hurt, pain and self-loathing. On my sober days I would think maybe this freedom thing is a possibility, but then rest assured the intoxication of self-doubt came quickly and reminded me of the impossibility of my reaching freedom. When I became sober again, between my intoxicated times I can also remember I would become frustrated and angry because it seems as though nothing was happening, nothing positive that is. But when it came to "church" time, I would just straighten myself up and I would act as though everything was ok. I wonder how many women and I am talking about "church going women" and even men too, are living the life of a lie. Maybe not to the extent and level which I did and maybe not even the same choice of poison, drug of choice, pain of choice, tormentor of choice, but you have something you need God's deliverance from. Maybe some of you are worse, in an even deeper pit than I was, but the message is still the same for all of us. Jesus saves, heals, delivers and sets free. God is a Deliverer.

Be assured that God is a Deliverer, I am talking about a knowing that comes from when you thought for sure you were going to go crazy, lose your mind and God stepped in. I am talking about if God didn't step in, you thought for sure that you could blow your brains out, or kill the person you were tied up with-where only God could sever the grip, or drive yourself over in the water and drown yourself, in the grips of Satan. (I thought about all these things) Praise is to the God of my salvation and deliverance.

Changed behavior by transformed thinking
Connected by sensory, my five senses of the natural man: see, hear, smell, taste and feel; then by the environment which I lived, my thoughts were formed. Circumstances, situations, habitual and addictive behavior also helped influenced them and my soulish realm, my mind and my thoughts offered Satan entry, access to control my very being, but then the Word of God came and gave me a different reference and this was when the battle internally began, the fight to the death of one or the other, but it would be the Word of God to change my thinking, it could be done no other way.

Think about the counsel of God: I am not going to take you out of the world; I'm going to have you overcome the world by the renewing of your mind through My Word by faith. (My summary).

Freedom, Healing and Deliverance had to take place because there was wounding and pain, deep sores in my soulish realm. I had wounded emotions. But Jesus brought to me Good Tidings, Good News, deliverance to Flora.

The Body of Christ still is experiencing bondage, we don't preach and teach Jesus enough; what He has done for us and who we are in Him. I was there in bondage to a mindset that would never allow you to be all that God has called you to be. I recognize the demon spirits. My faulty belief system produced faulty emotions and behavior. It took years for deliverance for me, but not for you, God is doing a quick work now. The wounding was lot of events, but the healing was a process. We allow invasions in our lives, which I did because I didn't know my value and I was a people pleaser, wanted acceptance at any cost. So I allowed misuse of myself both mentally and emotionally because of my faulty mindset and of course, thoughts and feelings naturally followed.
They were feelings of I didn't measure up; so I would work overtime on trying to please people, especially those I was seeking approval from. I always needed to have approval so this

distorted need put me in a position of misuse and abuse, not only by others but me also. Isn't that ironic you abuse yourself? The greatest abuse, torment and torture came from me, myself, my mind-my own mind beat me up more than anybody or anything else because it was an internal battle, I couldn't get away from it (except the un-thinkable) which some people do in order to hush or quiet the critic voice inside, the internal voices and the lies that they whisper. The battle was fierce, but God kept me through it. I love the "BUT GOD", aren't you glad for them too?

I allowed my boundaries, if there were any, I allowed what should have been there, boundaries to be violated and trespassed all because of the unhealthy need I had for approval, acceptance and validation; from outside sources. Then when that thing or person would move out of place and he did and often, at any given time, I would become distraught. I was co-dependent on another person's behavior and actions. I was ok if they were in place and not ok if they had moved out of place. I would feel inadequate and insignificant, unable to hold onto a relationship, I was not important enough. Then dysfunction would show up in a major way, which is passed from generation to generation, it is known as the thing to do in a family and no one prior to you have ever challenged the idea, the product of an un-renewed mind.

Abuse is allowed when value is not recognized, that **I am valuable, I am OK, I'm fantastic, I love myself and God loves me too.** These are my confessions now over me and my life, this is my belief system. Abuse is inevitable when value is not known or recognized; knowing your value is key. It will stop abuse in its tracks; it will say-NO. I learned that my needs don't cease or come into existence because of someone fulfilling them or not fulfilling them. God shattered that yoke, destroyed it, the yoke that held me in bondage to that "thought pattern". A thought pattern that was not only unhealthy it was destructive. We are held in bondage as long as our thought life is incorrect about a thing. The yoke was destroyed because of knowledge, which is the power of God's Word. Freedom and breakthrough occurred when my thought life, mindsets and perceptions of things changed. Amen. I could have never gone where my mind couldn't have taken me and being un-renewed it could not have taken me in the direction of wholeness and healing.

I desired freedom, but there was no space for it to happen, my mind's space was painfully packed with wrong thinking and freedom couldn't happen until my mind became renewed by God's Word, which created space for freedom, my habits of thinking and thoughts had to change and they did, then freedom was birthed.

In the past I came under condemnation spiritually because I thought I needed to endure everything, even abuse , the bad stuff, because I wouldn't be a "good Christian" if I didn't. After all, my identity was from what I did, not who I was in Christ. I worked hard at being good (remember the root cause of this thinking), the feeling of inadequacy. I needed acceptance and approval so how else do you get acceptance and approval? You get it by working hard, giving up your very being right? Wrong!!!!. I didn't think who I was –was OK, good enough. I went into works which served to injure me further. It made me feel bad, because guess what, after all that hard work to please, they still didn't give me acceptance or green lights, I would be devastated, felt worse than I did from the start. But the moment I became ok within myself, that yoke too was destroyed. It could not stand up against the knowledge I had come into, of the fact- THAT I AM OK. I am OK within myself.

I thought I had to make everything work out, (spirit of pride), it would cause me to be in the Lord's way, choosing my way and my understanding instead of His, this also keep me from trusting Him like I should. I was doing all the work…. We always think everything has to work out the way we think it should. But what is WORK OUT? Who says when something works out or not, who sets the standard for a thing working out? Isn't it based on what we think and what we think is colored by life's colors-the experiences we've had and what we have been told, that has been passed down from generation to generation without question, but isn't all is suppose to be entrusted to the Lord and trust Him for all outcomes, measuring them by His Word and His Word alone?

Good Christian or good person? Good Christians always fight to the bitter end, good Christians never quit and good Christians endure all and everything including the bad and the abusive stuff. This comes from a religious mindset, not God. God does not require us to take abuse. At the end of each day, He calls us to peace.

There are lessons in life and God promises to work things out for our good; Romans 8:32, but there is a lot involved in understanding what all this entails. I believe through interpretation by self and traditional teaching, we are subtly encouraged to take abuse, especially women; both socially and spiritually. We are trained from childhood, be nice, play nice and get along. These messages have caused us to stay in un-healthy relationships and places, physically, mentally and emotionally for too long. Some of these teachings were passed along silently without words, but heard at the same time through actions and perceived lifestyles of our parents and grandparents. They have caused in some areas severe damage and have caused us to be co-dependent upon bad behavior. We were taught to go with the "flow" so to speak. It is better to be seen and not heard, so my voice, and your voice were silenced through learned behavior early on in life by flawed and erroneous teachings and concepts of life lived by others, this lifestyle we accepted as truth so we conformed to these teachings as the guide for our thinking. Secondly, do we over interpret the bible because of what we need it to say, to justify, or to explain the reason to what we are doing, thinking or living when it really is fear that keeps us from moving on.

Other Times:
There were times during my journey when I would be angry also at my superiors and sometimes at the companies I worked for. I would express it negatively by talking with other employees,

whoever was present. This attitude came from the wounding and anger I had along the way while on the journey to healing and wholeness. From not realizing that I had the power to achieve my own success, I had the key to it; God had given it to me, which it had been up to me all along. Blinded by an inadequate self-portrait of myself, I thought others were the source of my discontentment, I viewed them as such and I realize now, that as long as I was viewing someone else (outside) of me for my discontentment and the block to my success and happiness, I would never become free of man's opinions as long as I held on the belief that they held the key to my success. The beliefs I had about them kept me from accepting responsibility for myself. I always thought that someone else outside of me held the key and blocked the pathway to my greatness.

This perception of them generated by my mindset was a false one. This was the source of my bondage, not an external thing or person outside and it kept me locked into a perpetual anger, which was extremely destructive and to follow that was resentment, it also served to keep me in a unsuccessful place, and it kept my focus on wrong thinking.

Fear….., after being emotionally messed up I learned to mask my feelings, I learned not to feel and I learned not to trust because of the wounding and hurt. I distrusted my feelings and emotions, and in doing so I also shut down the ability to be led by the Holy Spirit of God; because it is an inward witness He leads us by. I didn't trust anything I could feel from within. I was quick to follow external things still. I learned to act though, but I was calling it strength, but it was not strength it was fear. Fear of rejection, not being accepted. Feared to trust, I feared getting hurt again which meant I was still trying to manage my pain and sustaining myself instead of giving it all to the Lord and trust that He was able to take care of me and protect me. The weight of it was too much for me to bear, but I tried. I had shut down on feeling and this had caused me also not to live to the fullest God desired for me. His leadings by the inward witness and of His Presence became stifled.

I missed God so many times. I was waiting for some verbal, a thunder bolt or a prophet or somebody to tell me what God needed to say to me. Instructions to do this or do that, but God had given me His Spirit to hear Him. Today July 20th, 2004, I surrendered all that I had of myself and ever hoped to be to God. I surrendered my life. I now live a life of hope in Christ Jesus.
I became free, no longer concerned or consumed by life's issues. I surrendered all, I realized that even though I loved God with all my heart, soul, mind and strength; and everything within me, I was still living two lives, my life had not become "ONE" with Him, my Master, Christ. Well now it's "ONE" with Him. Amen….

I surrendered and Lord I repent (turned away) from the double life. I realized by your "GRACE" how controlling I was, controlling of my own life, (heard what I said right-"my life") Yeah right- I had not released myself to God. I thought I had and I bet you think you have too, but in all truth and actuality you probably haven't either. I don't have a life anymore, what I live, the life that I live now is faith in the Son of God. Even though I was doing all the right things and loving God, however, the Holy Spirit chose to reveal an even greater "Truth" to me, thank You Holy Spirit, without You we would walk in darkness in every area of our lives, thank You for Your Light, which You shine upon and into our lives. He allowed me to see myself in the light of God's Word, the life of Christ.

Can I tell anyone that at fourteen years (it was at that time) from when the Lord drew me to re-dedicate my life to Him, that I had totally surrendered myself, my life to God; no, I had not, if it had not been revealed to me I wouldn't have known either. I know we talk about being sold-out, but are we really sold-out? To the Lord that is, because some of us are sold-out, but to other things, but not to our God and our Lord. Now I have surrendered, given my **other** life to Christ. I resigned as CEO-Chief Executive Officer of my life.

It was a spirit of pride, always working and looking to myself for answers and the keeping of myself as I mentioned in earlier paragraphs and remember the root cause of this spirit is "Fear" the need to control, but it produces failure, it bears no good fruit, no prosperity in the things of God. I am not talking about not being responsible, but I'm talking about the obsessive need to control because of fear. The need to control kept me from moving forward and probably caused me to miss some blessings I'm sure.

The reason for this story, my brothers and sisters is that; I was saved, but controlled by flawed and defective thinking. These same spirits, attitudes and lifestyles are active in the "church" today. Bondage in the church, going to church Sunday after Sunday, Wednesday after Wednesday, every time the church door opens-we're there and secretly being tormented within from bondages.

The oppressed mind, the way we think and the way I thought........

I know that life and circumstances have lied to you. They have told you that you are doomed and what you are experiencing is what you will have to experience forever, that this is your fate; it has been assigned to you. There is nothing you can do; there is no hope, so just give up, throw in the towel. (Continue to live defeated)

These circumstances were in line with the lies above that Satan was feeding to your mind. So you think and cannot see anything different, you thought it was truth, no matter how bad it was and got.
Satan was and is allowed to touch your circumstances, but fear not, it is all working out for your good. I am here to tell you that Satan is a liar, he is simply not the truth; God's Word is Truth for your life. The Truth, God's Word says that He has a plan for you, to do good and not evil, to give you an expected end, one of Hope, Life, Joy and Love in the power of the Holy Spirit. Hold

onto this Word. God has life for you and He wants to give it to you. Now the choice is yours, it was mine, God loves us so much that He did not leave us without a choice, the Comforter-Holy Spirit someone to be with us always and He did not even withhold His very own Son Jesus from us, what kind of love is this saints……So we can make a choice, we have the power to do so…Amen

He sent His Son Jesus and His Holy Spirit that if you believe in Him you will not be left hurting, wounded and bleeding on the inside. He shed His blood for you so that you would not have to be without "HELP". The Comforter He is. So let's take a moment to invite Him in, to cast off all restrains that are holding you back and relinquish, let go of the old man and let's put on the new man which is created after God.

There is much the Lord wants to reveal to you. I am telling you this because this is what He has done for me. No one could have told me that I would ever be whole. See I know the battle, I know and I understand what it is like to have to secretly suffer and be tormented by the enemy of our souls.
But one thing I did learn is that he is no match for our God and the end is already fixed. It has to happen the way it is suppose to and that is for your good. God has promised it and God can not lie, He is not man that He should tell a lie. Much, much does God have for you.

CHAINS BROKEN

September 2006-2007, another time and season when it was one of the most trying times of my life. Even the truth about and of God was questioned and tested beyond measure it seemed. God brought me through though, then the season changed and revelation understanding of God and who He is and who He is in my life unfolded and began to flow and pour into my life like a river without banks or boundaries. Unlimited in the amount of revelation knowledge, no limit of God revealing Himself to me. I began to experience God in ways like never before. I became all that God had created me to be, I began to believe and grab a hold of the fact that I was not wrong in my personhood, that God had a purpose and plan for my life, even though I had heard this and probably knew it on some level, I finally really believed it. I was not wrong in my personhood, bad breaks in life, failed relationships, promotions desired, but did not receive, pains, hurts and wounds, but I was not wrong in my personhood, who I was. I was not wrong in the "real" me, my spirit, which was born-again of a Perfect God, my Father. It was only in my soulish realm that I had been held captive by falsehood and distorted thoughts and views.

My mess had a purpose, I wasn't crazy and there was nothing wrong with me. Now this subject will take weeks and months and maybe even years for me to share it all with you; but I want to share as much as possible because I want you to be free. I don't want you to hurt and have all this pain and think there is no one who understands you out there. Well I am here to tell you I do, I understand because I was once there. I had shame, I felt ashamed, I had to suffer in the closet and I had to act like everything was ok. You know that pretty package all wrapped up, but has broken glass inside of it, (your heart).

I believed the lie; you know the lie that Satan through circumstances and the experiences I experienced, you know those voices. This was my own battle for as long as I can remember, since I had been saved and walking with God.
The mind, would I ever be free or was this assigned as my fate for

life was always the question? I summed it all up like Solomon said in Ecclesiastes, It wasn't just happening to me, there was nothing new under the sun, there was nothing wrong with me (besides my thinking at the time), there was nothing wrong with me why I was or seemed to be doomed to experiencing what I thought had come to destroy me but rather what I was and had been experiencing was common to all those who are called and chosen of God.

The nature of the "Offense" realized, July 2007, I had believed the lie as I said before, then the promises of God came, then the disappointment of what seemed as though the promises were not coming through. Then the offense came and then the wounding from self-pity came. I lived years, more and more of them in what I would call or describe as a deep wounding. The wounding came because of all the wrong viewpoints I had. I could not see or understand if God said He could and would do all these things, why they weren't happening for me. I was hurting and bleeding to death.

I went through so much; I was seriously confused at this dilemma. I became angry and depressed with life and with God because I knew that He had the power and the ability to stop this hurt, pain and confusion, so why was He not doing it. That led from disappointment to anger, to offense to wounding. After all, He had promised me peace of mind, strength and most of all freedom, which I yearned and craved to no end. I needed freedom like I needed air to breathe, food to eat and water to drink. Didn't He see this and know this? Of course He did and He was doing something about it, it was the enemy of my soul that was blinding me and keeping me from realizing that truth.

I couldn't understand if God was God and He never lies, why then He allowed husband after husband, boyfriend after boyfriend to leave, when He knew that was where I was looking for my affirmation and acceptance from. (See how wise God is). He knew if man gave it to me, then man could take it away.

It wasn't until one Wednesday I had tuned into Noel Jones and he was ministering on the "Offense". He said if you don't trip (give up) you will receive the blessing (breakthrough) mentally and spiritually in your soul, you would be set free.

This was the turning point; this was the anointed word that broke and destroyed the yoke of that thought pattern. It was a yoke I had been living under for quite some time, thinking that it was going to be that way forever. That word about "offense" came and he kept it real. He put it just like it is, as it had been with me.

It has been 22 years since I embarked on this journey with Lord, but He who has begun a good work will complete it until the day of Jesus Christ's return. Still having my mind renewed daily, but I can tell you God is faithful and He is a Deliverer. I share with you the goodness of the Lord, His mercy and His grace, which all of which is who He is, amen.

The battle against your mind has been the battle to retrain your thinking. Old mindset against the new. I now identify with Christ, not the things of the world through sensory and perception of them. (What I can see and or experience). My identity is one with Christ; the experiences that I have experienced do not define me or determine my future. They do not determine who I am or cause me to be something that God did not create or call me to be.

I am a woman of God, called and sanctified for His glory. The experiences, while real have been used by God and will still be for His glory and my good. They did not always reveal the best that God had for me, instead they lied to me. They told me I was someone else or something else besides God's divine purpose for me and my life; but God delivered me.

The way we think, view, perceive and do things all are controlled by the mind. The way we think will determine if I'm going to be happy, sad, have joy or be miserable. Choices, oh the choices we have.

My story after years, countless books, writings and tablets filled of revelations; I realize that it was my mind. My thoughts and the patterns of them were all arriving from the place of the mind. I realize that my perception was off, way off; I thought everything had come to destroy me. I would love to say I had faith and it just zapped it all away, but it didn't happen that way. Part of the reason for this was I didn't believe in myself and trust the guidance that God promised; I didn't have the trust and the faith in my decisions and the unctions of my spirit by Holy Spirit. Because I thought I could never do anything great for fear of making a mistake or that I would fail at it, so I did nothing, or should I say I dabbled at the edge of the water of life, dipping my desire for freedom in once and a while, but I dared not go out into the deep. After all it would defy everything I thought about myself, everything I been told, everything I thought through that old stinking thinking, everything that the "Doom Sayers" had either said verbally or insinuated through their actions.

I was controlled by it all; I dared not go into the deep of total freedom. Throw caution to the wind and away to follow the leading of the Holy Spirit. See I would quench the leading of the Spirit because of fear and self-doubt. For fear it was just me dreaming big, visioning great things. I would rationalize it saying it was just my mind inflated, after all, I was nobody, who would believe me or care about what I thought? I feared it was just me, my own voice, because for the majority of my life I felt the feeling of being insignificant. That it was just my way of conjuring up and dreaming up some over inflated ideas, but they were my dreams, they were true dreams, dreams and visions given to me by my Heavenly Father. Because these were the things He wanted to use to impact the world through me. It was God trying to lead me, but because of the conditioning of my mind (my thinking) I had both learned and come to expect nothing great of myself.

Nothing great could ever come from me or about me right? I wanted safety and surety because I feared. It was simply fear, nothing else. I was battling with what I knew (the old mindset) verses what was possible in God and a new mindset. I had been brain-washed, conditioned by the life I had lived. I had been brain-washed and it was life, we learn what we live. I am remembering the failed relationships, unfulfilled dreams, requests not granted, these were a few of the things that were used to influence the failure mindset.

The failed relationships formed and made manifest the hidden, suppressed and undeveloped emotional state of being I was in. They also revealed wounds that showed up through behaviors from the self-destructive mindset. Thinking that I was a failure because the relationships failed or should I say didn't last. I don't know if they were supposed to last or not last. I was naïve, I did not know so I became wounded in my soul and my emotions. These failed relationships sent that message to me that there must be something "wrong" that was supposed to be "right". Where was I drawing this reference from? An unholy source…. But now I know I can do all things through Christ who strengthens me.

I am powerful now in the things of God and my life with a new mindset and now I empower my daughter, lead her into the "Truth", the Truth of God's Word and the truth about herself. That she is a beautiful and wonderful young lady and let no one, nobody take that from her or rob her of the joy of knowing it.
I teach her that she is worthy of good and genuine love. That she was created worthy of these things, but because of the enemy of our souls they sometime become distorted along the way. But thanks are unto God who is a Deliverer through Jesus Christ, His Son. We were created worthy.

You see, before I couldn't see this for the life of me, I couldn't recognize and grasp the fact that I was worth more, that I was created to be more than what I was living and experiencing at the time. That I had value and worth, but because of my lack of knowledge Satan had victory, because of that lack I also perished for a while and a while.

Flora Samuel

After being racked and ravaged by pain and self-pity for such a long time, I would become worn out, tired and sometimes bitter and that occasionally caused the offense at God to creep in again. This was when the Lord lifted me up, when all was forsaken He was there, but I couldn't see through my pain and discouragement. By this time I think I had earned a P.H.D. in discouragement, wounding, self-pity and self-doubt, I was blinded by it all; but God was faithful. I will teach and share with every woman my journey and I will inform them, remind them of their worth and value and educate them about the tactics and devices of the enemy of their wholeness and their greatness.

Satan sets out early on in life to destroy us and distort our God-given need for love, acceptance and to belong. He camouflages the path God has called us to and laid out before us. To replace our natural yearnings for fulfillment of all things good, for the things of this world. I recognize it; it was the hand of the enemy trying to keep me from reaching where I am now, today and where I am going to be in the future. I could not understand again for the life of me what was happening to me, things I thought should not have happen, things I didn't even know existed, after all, I was twenty-five years of age before I knew that someone would lie to you. I didn't know drugs existed until I was about twenty years old; I had a sheltered and unprepared life. I had nothing to draw reference from for the things that was happening to me, so I definitely thought that they had come to destroy. I can remember one time at a meeting I was crying out have mercy Lord, have mercy Lord, have mercy, I was so new in the faith at that time, and that was all I knew. I knew I needed help, so I asked for His mercy.

What makes us not trust ourselves? Especially as women, is it the failures, the mistakes of the past or is it mainly the things we perceived as failures keep us from trusting ourselves. We say to ourselves that nothing has worked for me before, so I better not try this or try that, it may fail too, what will people say and think? "Self-Doubt" never allowed us to trust ourselves.

It is like forgiveness, everybody tells you to forgive this one and forgive that one, but nobody tells you to forgive yourself, which is paramount. Well trusting ourselves is the same concept. We are taught to trust our parents, our teachers, our bosses and the list goes on and on, but little is taught on one of the most important things we can learn to do in our lives and that is to trust ourselves. Especially when your life is a committed life to God. As women were not taught to trust ourselves, but we don't blame anybody now and we believe that our parents did the best they could with what they knew and now we have choices, no matter what hand life dealt us, we can be different and we choose to be different and we choose to be victorious at doing it…. Our pathway to greatness has been un-blocked by the knowledge we have come into….. That I can do all things through Christ who strengthens me……. Amen and Amen, so be it…..

We were not always told that we are beautiful, but it doesn't matter how beautiful you actually are physically if your heart belongs to the Lord, because you are the "Apple" of His eye. You are His Beloved and He is yours….. Before I came into this knowledge I was prey to men that saw me as prey, because I was seeking for love in all the wrong places, being full of self doubt and feeling unvalued. Self-Doubt had been on the journey with me for about 17 years, I didn't believe anything good could happen for me, even with God and His blessing me. I still had to fight, I must still now, to the present time be alert for the temptation of being self-doubtful or to have the activity of that spirit in my life.

That spirit would cause me to look at others and compare myself to them. I would measure myself how well or how well not I was doing or being. Every time I did "that" compare myself or measure myself on the "supposedly" ladder or yard stick of success, I came up short every time, because I had glorified and mystified others and their positions because they headed up huge ministries. On the other end I was still drawing men who would further injure me, yes there were a few of them over the years. Emotionally unavailable ones, just plain ole un-unavailable ones, ones that simply didn't care to be anything other than what they were being, who they were, the ones with un-developed character and yes ladies I am talking about the ones in church also, those knocking down the door every time there was service, they were "men of God", but sent satanically, because their fleshly appetites were not put to death yet and they were not under the Holy Spirit's control yet.

I now trust and follow the leading of the Holy Spirit by reading God's Word, when He impresses things upon my spirit I know it is Him, I now expect God to speak; He speaks and now I listen. I doubted myself in the past and it has caused me to lose some time and ground, but God is able to restore unto me the youth of my years and the years that the canker worm and palmer worm, (life situations) have stolen from me. I now try to follow in absolute and total obedience to faith by the leading of God by His Spirit. Wherever He leads, I will follow…

Don't let persecution keep you in the need to be in control because persecution is normal for the believer as long as they are here on the earth; which is fallen in its state. The need to control is an enemy of faith; it blinds the view of God in our lives to the point that only self is seen and at that point others who need to see God in your life can't because only self is in view.

Self Pity- Wounded Spirits- Jesus has healing for life's hurts, living a joyful life regardless of life's circumstances and situations; cooperating with Holy Spirit is the key…. The sin of self-pity is one of the devastating enemies of our soul, it is a self-centered mindset that takes our focus off the Lord and put it onto ourselves, which is the gateway for Satan to enter our thoughts.

Over time I internalized this craving for approval and I learned to idolize others at my own expense. This became a pattern in my love relationships. Now as an adult, I would re-create this scenario by giving my love partners all of my power, elevating them above myself. Re-creating those old familiar yearnings I

grew accustomed to as a child feeling emotionally deprived and less-than and less-than is what I had come to expect. I was used against my own self, the destroying would come from within, I didn't feel ok in my own skin and I thought everybody else felt the same way about me; so I allowed preconceived thoughts of my own-what I thought others thought about me cause me to fear.
Fear tends to incubate, gaining intensity over time. Insecurity which was learned from childhood increases with each rejection whether it is romantic or not. It caused me to look to others for something I didn't know how to give myself. I would seek approval from my lovers and husbands, recreating an already damaged mindset, learned as a child, even from my grandmother who resented the position of caregiver for us, her grandchildren. My mom worked and lived in the neighboring town. Another rejection and abuse by a grandmother, who resented my mom for being the only child still remaining out of her two children. She resented my mom for being alive still because her beloved son died at an early age around 42 years old. So that hatred and rejection was passed onto me, my grandmother took her frustrations out on me; I had two other sisters, which were my mother and grandmother's favorites. This could go so many places, but enough for now, you get the picture-right? Huh-heavy…..

Conversely, after that I was unable to feel anything when someone freely admired me or wanted to love me or appreciate me, because I felt I needed to work for it, to earn it, like I had learned to live and act out as a child. This carried over into my spiritual life, my walk with the Lord, my Heavenly Father, how He could freely love me, allowed His Son to die for me and to freely give me all things through Him. I was performance oriented, I needed to be good in order to get good, to be accepted, and I had to behave a certain way in order to be approved of. Boy, did God have a work on His hands, right? And only He could fix it, I spent years on fixing myself, to make myself good enough, adequate enough, to make myself "OK" for others and myself, for the sick-distorted mindset I had created for myself.

Flora Samuel

My Question- Where do I go from here?

It wasn't until this year, I received a full revelation of, I am totally forgiven and completely loved. Now I have known this for years, but it is quite extraordinary when the Holy Spirit comes along and reveals it to you. It consumes you and helps you to know that it is really real and it is Truth for you, not just in the Scriptures, but for you personally. It causes praise from deep within you, your core, what it really means to know that you are totally forgiven, accepted and completely loved. Now this may not mean much to everybody, but to a person like me, who God has had to work overtime on, when it came to deliverance, then you understand where I'm coming from. Let's hear it from the Redeemed, from the Delivererees....... Amen

Another time, this was one of the times used by Holy Spirit to continue His work on me and through me. I had reached this point in my early fifties, I found myself still struggling to find my place in society, in a world which I knew was in desperate need of what God had placed in me and that I had it to offer. Had God allowed me to be born and saved for me to be frustrated? So you can imagine at this point in life I had become very frustrated. My frustration level had reached an all-time high. This was one of those times when all the reading, pep talk and even praying seemed useless. Plus my energy level had reached an all time low.

I had no energy therefore I had no motivation and with no motivation I seemed even more helpless and drained. I was drained mentally, emotionally and definitely physically. My mind was tired and my physical systems were too. I had knots in the back of my neck and swollen glands from the tension and this was all giving indication of my frustration level.
Where do you find yourself at this time in your life? Are you zooming through life enjoying all it has to offer or are you struggling to stay alive mentally and every other way also?

My question was to God, my Maker, my Creator, who according to His Word and I believe it, created me in His own likeness and His very own image. So if that is the "Truth", the facts and basis for which I am to be and see myself, what happened then?

Now to add to the mix, age and time are speeding my way, so adding those dynamics and elements to the mix; I had come to the explosive point. (You can have explosive points in this walk). So don't be alarmed if it happens. The lid is bubbling up from the pressure of the mixture. What do I do? Where do I go from here? There were not enough well-wishing friends or acquaintances to help me over this one. I had reached the point where I couldn't even tell my friends, I didn't know if I even had any real friends at that time. I was questioning everything. I couldn't tell anyone for fear that they would not understand the extreme extent of the matter that I needed them to understand. Would they think I was crazy? Even the church made me live a lie, I was in hiding. There was no one to tell, no one to go to. To say I am hurting, I need you, I need help no one to turn to. Who could I tell, I wasn't feeling like going to God, because I was tired, that would take lots of work, remember, I thought I had to work and earn things from God like everybody else.

After all, the church (worldwide) had created and become a false place, it was not for the real at heart; it was for those who pretended everything was "OK", isn't that what they tell you while you are bleeding to death on the inside? So where do I go from here? That's my question-right? Yes.......

I had been going through this off and on for almost 15 years at the time of deliverance, under extreme conditions with periodic saneness breaks. Is it just a case of my reality, my belief system? Or are there some real forces working themselves against my greatness, my being or have I set myself up?

Have I learned or created a picture of myself of what or how I am suppose to be at this point and the point before now? Could this be what is making me discouraged and disappointed in myself? Am I looking at myself and then looking at others and coming up with a conclusion that I have missed the mark. Who says I'm not

"OK" where I am and who I am for right now. Um?

What's the proof to support my logic of thinking, "what is wrong with me"? Why am I not yet teaching the masses? Is it my time or has my time passed me by? Are the answers to these and all other questions found in love, the Word, the God of the Word or what or where? What is it? What am I looking for? What do I want to be-what do I want to do? Will I recognize it if I become it? Will I be satisfied when and if I got there to that place and where is that place, is it way out and far beyond this point where I am right now, or is it already here? Am I already there? Just where is it that I am trying to go?

Did I want more money, a better position; being someone of importance (my perception of what is important). Wear new tailored clothing, look important, have people pay attention to me. Did I want power? Just what is it? What is it that I wanted? Did I want to be a leader, which I was born to be and I believed that with all my heart. These are all the questions I asked myself, I knew all these questions were the cause of my frustrations because I was not "Resting" in the Lord, leaving all to Him. I was also surrounded by people who did not recognize my talents and who I was at my very core, my soul. This was hard, all of it, with all the questions.

Then I had to create this image what seems like my entire life, this other person to be able to cope mentally. I had allowed others to create a place for me in life based on what they wanted or didn't want from me. I allowed them to be the carving knife and the decision maker for my shape in life. These things I realize today had never allowed me to be myself. I had to create different images and personalities for "fitness" into a society and world and don't forget the "church world" was in there too, worlds that were not comfortable with me being me. Hey, but no finger pointing at them, because I wasn't comfortable with all the greatness God had placed in me. I was in my weakened state, my learned frame of reference from childhood, the belief system which in turn helped create my realities.

It is now today August 2006, I had to go back to the drawing board to "define" Flora, myself. Who was she? Did I still know who she was? Underneath the maze of distorted images of others' creations; of my own creations; could I find her? Would I like her and welcome her? Living the standard of integrity that I had to secretly live, not having the courage to be myself and openly live it out because I had to become someone else to live in the worlds that did not know me and I wasn't sure if they wanted to know me. Because that person-"the real person" who Flora is, would not allow them to remain the way they were living, who they were; especially if they were not living the standard I knew was possible, if they had not reached this level of integrity and character.

Was it this place I was afraid to live; did I fear this place, because of my need to be accepted and wanted; for people to approve of me, had it kept me from living in this level of integrity (remember the sickness-sacrificing and compromising to be accepted). Did my need to be accepted over power my call to stand in this level?

Since at this level I would not be understood as much and as badly as I wanted to be (in my sickness), the bondage mindset. Again a memory from my childhood is surfacing at the moment. I remember my grandmother's resentment and hatred toward me, how she showed it through isolating me, thus making me feel alienated from my all loved two sisters by her, both of whom she showered with acceptance.

My torment now was to walk in boldness this incredible sacrificial way of life of integrity or to be accepted and understood. So which would it be, which one would win out, I never thought I would be strong enough to stand against this distorted mindset. It was wrong and I was made wrong from childhood in my thinking. But thanks be to God, I am no longer bound by such crippling mindsets. I have been set free. Praise is to God, my Father, the Lord Jesus Christ and the power of Holy Spirit…..

As time happened I found myself knowing that there is something different and more than I've known and experienced, no more church as usual, no more anything as usual, but mostly church. I found myself that I no longer wanted to go to church; I could not stomach it any more in the state I had witnessed it in. Didn't exactly know why yet, not exactly sure. Was I supposed to start my own ministry that God had called me to at this time or what? I began to see more clearly the revelation of Christ even more than that I was reading from the bible. The Holy Spirit would reveal things to me, I was not sure what it all meant at the time, but I knew I had to do something.

I had begun to have new thoughts, I could envision the supernatural of myself doing unusual things or should I say things that the normal church was not doing, not even discussing. I am saying Lord, what is this? They were just regular and routine as usual. I knew with everything in me that it was lacking and falling short of the great price of God's Son, Christ Jesus and even falling short and lacking in what I had come to know by God's Spirit. I felt as though I was on the verge of doing something different (by ordinary church standards); I was on the verge of doing something extraordinary; I felt it in me; **it was pushing and driving me.**

I am about to give birth to something and I don't know where to go to have this baby. I am about to have a spiritual birth of some sort, but don't know where to go and have it. Still the same question; where do I go from here…..

I do not know anyone I can talk to or anyone experiencing the leading of the Spirit also that knows something is about to happen, that has not happen during our lifetime, not in the history of recent Christendom. I was not going to ask for anyone's buy-in; at this point God had healed me from the need to have man's approval or acceptance.

I just need direction where to go to have birth. Are you in a place or church and you know God is calling you to a new place, but you are not sure what to do or where to go? Well, Jesus was born in obscurity, not in a great and notable place. There is no room in the Inn? (The Church), literally to bring forth this new and fresh wine of Your Spirit Lord, so Father where do I go to give birth of this special baby? Give birth to the things of God.

Do I just start talking, telling everybody who I come across or anybody who will listen to what I believe is a move of God, or do You have a special place Lord for your baby to be born? I am not to fear anything or anybody? Viewing the church world and its condition stronger or greater than You God within me. I am remembering the two spies that came back with a faith-filled report-I too have one, I am through Christ well able to bring about the delivery of this baby…..(Message)……. Amen

Is the church sewed up and fortified by its current leaders to the point it cannot be penetrated for God to bring forth His new wine- the fresh move of His Spirit? Is this the perception I have, they have? Like the city of Jericho, the people thought they were impenetrable, but they were not, right…. Lord I don't know how this can be done, but You do. Lord I trust You to make the way of this birth…. Amen

Rejection and intimidation-two really evil spirits, but they will not keep me from delivering this baby, this Word…., I resist the spirits of rejection and intimidation in the name of Jesus. I will not fear in Jesus' name…….

The key was, don't make it our position and goal in life to be understood. It is a basic and fundamental need for the human race, but you can't make it your life's goal. So if I was going to go forth with delivery I could not be afraid and yearn for acceptance and understanding from others. I had to do what God was doing through me. The enemy will use your un-controlled and unhealthy desires for acceptance and to be understood against you, especially with a person like myself, before deliverance. Trying to be understood is the by-product, the working out of the fear of rejection. You are thinking if they just get to know me, those were my thoughts, which only leads to people-pleasing, into "WORKS". You think don't they know I am a good person? It forces you to become an idolater and a very frustrated one; because it will become so that enough is never going to be enough, so don't become a slave to it, to the person, leader, or the church to avoid the possibility of them rejecting you. Personally we try to get their affections, and on other levels approval and acceptance.

This is a evil spirit it tried to revisit me (familiar spirits) through a new job, new boyfriend, new husband, an inadequate spirit, the spirit of an inferior complex, a mental spirit, because it was aware of my incorrect picture I had of myself in the past. That I would sabotage my own future and opportunities, whether it was to minister the Gospel of Jesus Christ or simply an employment opportunity, no matter what it was, that spirit would count on me in assisting in my own downfall by my mindset about the thing. All the demon spirit needed to do was to make me doubt through a spoken word by someone or even by myself, to place doubt upon who I was in Christ and who He is in me. The evil spirit knew that he only needed to place doubt in my mind through the actions or lack of them of another (realize they are external and have no power over me internally unless I give it to them), but I would give it power, I would water it and tend to it by giving it my attention, by allowing it to occupy my mind and my thoughts.

All these things you were never told in church and you didn't dare share yours; after all, we had an image to uphold, while in bondage and bleeding to death in secret. Right? We desperately try and want to hold onto things, because we think and feel that our happiness is tied up into this thing or this person. I learned that my joy and happiness is not contingent on this thing or that thing, or any other person outside of me in my life. It is Christ and Him alone to fulfill those positions.

I am going to be happy and have joy whether or not this thing is in my life or I'm not with this person, because life is not based on them. God is the source of my life; this is where I am now, but not then.
I gripped onto every man that had been in my life for dear life, because I was afraid if they left or were no longer in my life; I would not and could not be happy. A lie from the pit of hell, a thought from an un-renewed mind. I was held captive by my own thoughts. But, now I am happy even if this man, this thing, this job, or whatever is not there, because it is none of those things anyway.... It was God to bring about peace, joy and love I had for so many long, long and desperate years tried to find, and to God be the glory...... He gave me all when He gave me Jesus...Amen

I, not someone else did this, desperately tried to hold onto people who didn't want to be held onto; because I had connected my happiness to them, it was dependent upon being with them. Satan uses things like these un-healthy attachments, soul-ties to keep us bound and unfruitful to the work of the ministry, which is not God's plan for us. I became so engrossed and focused on making these relationships work until I became possessed with working them out. I was going insane; doing things I would have never done if I was healthy, mentally and emotionally in my thinking. I had become a slave to my distorted passions and desires, so the enemy used this as a continuous open door and built strongholds in my mind to keep me in bondage.

I would grip these men so hard until it scared them to death, they ran for the hills the first break they got and looking back I don't blame them. I was trying to make gods out of them, when they were totally incapable of ensuring my every moment of happiness; they did not want that responsibility, they ran for cover.....
I was saying to them you are my happiness and they were saying through their actions no I am not.

July 2010, later on in a few more chapters, I had funeral service for all below.

I began to cancel assignments of words, controlling behaviors of others that had caused me to pattern myself, to live my life, to behave a certain way, which had created mindsets for me. I cancel them now in the name of Jesus.

I took authority, assignments cancelled in Jesus' name. Words that had been spoken over me from infancy to childhood, from childhood to adulthood, words I'm aware of and those I'm not aware of, but God is, I cancelled their assignments in Jesus' name.

Every word that had been spoken negatively about me-released in the atmosphere, I cancelled them in the name of Jesus; every word that had been spoken and caused me to form opinions and mindsets about myself that are negative and against God's perfect plan for my life and destiny of it, I commanded it destroyed, null and void in Jesus' name.

Every word and assignment that is not godly, not positive in launching me into what God had called me to do, I cancelled it in Jesus' name. Every label is and was removed in Jesus' name and every influence was broken in the name of Jesus, every door was shut, closed in Jesus' name.

I will never again be controlled by the actions or the lack of them from others. I cancelled attachments, soul-ties, habits, mindsets and behaviors that were contrary to the will and best for my life in God, in Jesus' name.

By learning to stop allowing my self-esteem to be dependent on external sources, I was able to start taking responsibility and control for my feelings and the quality of my life experiences. That allowed me to stop trying to control and manipulate the men in my life and others because I thought they had the power over my feelings and happiness; it also allowed me to stop being an emotional vampire and from being that always needy woman.

I also started nurturing myself even the more spiritually, which was nurturing emotionally at the same time. I was able to stop looking to others to fill the hole I felt within. I stopped being so emotionally starved, which made me stop blaming others for my unhappiness and my emotional sadness. **"I became "HONEST" with myself"**.

By learning to separate my emotional reactions from my self-worth I was able to stop reacting, to the place of living and responding from a healthier place. I started separation between myself and other people comparatively. I started to see my self-worth as separate from my feelings and I began to place my value and self-worth in Christ and in what He had done for me. This all allowed me to stop judging myself and to forgive myself and others. I began to separate the natural from the spiritual, so then I began to live the "limitless life". I recognized that I was not without power to live this limitless life and I was not going to be passive about living it…

Another revelation for me, you think what is happening to you is because of you, but it's not, it's a humanity thing and experience, so don't allow the enemy to bring you under condemnation and convince you something is wrong with you or you did something wrong. Don't let self-pity take control of your mind, the enemy just wants you to become discourage and most of all, deem God unfaithful.

Surrender all, no more excuses for lame situations, lying by the pool of life waiting for something to happen. We speak to and command life to come forth; we've been in our crippled situations far too long. We no longer wait for someone to come and stir the waters for us, we do it ourselves… Amen

God is certainly moving us into the mature perfect man in Christ and our mindsets are as such, we no longer say what I will to do, I don't and that I don't want to do, I do. We thank the Lord for a life above that, thank You Lord we are no longer in the survival mode, we have abundance and we are able to share blessings with others....I gave birth, it was a battle and the only way the battle was won was by standing on God's Word; and I won……..

𝔉𝔲𝔫𝔢𝔯𝔞𝔩 𝔖𝔢𝔯𝔳𝔦𝔠𝔢 today for bad thoughts, hurt feelings, bad memories, disappointments, offenses and whatever that had a negative influence in your life.

They (all those bad feelings and tormentors) lived a long and must say a somewhat successful life, but today I said "NO MORE", I am taking control, I decided today, right now they were not good company.

So today (date) _____, I (your name) _____ put to rest everything I have brought to mind, named and listed on this paper and things I did not name, everything that has caused me to form an opinion about myself that is contrary to the Word of God for me and my life.

I cancel assignments, words, controlling behaviors of myself and others that have caused me to pattern myself, live my life, behave a certain way and everything that I have allowed to create mindsets for me, I cancel and bury them now, today in the name of Jesus.

Assignments cancelled, words that have been spoken over me from infancy to childhood, from childhood to adulthood; words that I am aware of and those I am not aware of, but God is, **I cancel them now today,** in Jesus' name.

Every word that has been spoken negatively about me, even if I have spoken them myself-that was released into the atmosphere; I cancel them now in the name of Jesus.

Every word that has been spoken and caused me to form opinions and mindsets about myself that are negative, against God's perfect plan for my life and my destiny. I command it destroyed, null and void in Jesus' name. Amen, Amen.....

I put to rest today, once and for all; labels that have been placed on and over my life, even if it has been done by me, to determine my destiny or allow it to control or influence me and the decisions I make after today for my life.....
Any and all influences that; they had, have been cancelled and laid to rest today, never to return again Jesus' name.... Amen...

You will no longer live according to the dictates of negative influences, no matter their origins (where they came from).

No longer will you be controlled by the actions or thoughts **or the lack of them** (approval) from others; they no longer have the power to influence your day or destiny for the worst...

When the temptation (old way of thinking) tries to re-visit you (in your thoughts) - **You will refuse it** & remind it & yourself of its death and burial..... Amen....Amen....

Remember our words-which is our confession must agree with our desired results for a thing!!!!   Amen…..

This is not a sad event; it's a "JOYOUS" ONE, one of DELIVERANCE AND JOY TO THE HIGHEST!!!!!

<u>List</u> all the things you are burying today, <u>do not reason</u> anything, <u>list it.</u>

<u>NOW,</u>
<u>I forgive myself, forgive yourself as Christ has done and we make the conscious decision to move forward today</u>

DO NOT RESUSCITATE

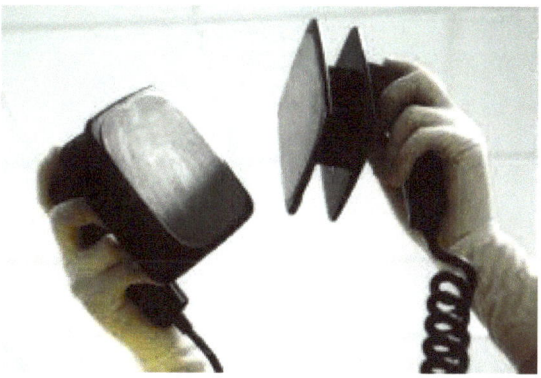

Have you been reviving your issues?

Are you ready to finally be done with **"That"**?

What do you do when what you thought was dead is still living on life support.

In Psalms, David said "I pursued my enemies and didn't turn back until they were consumed".

It is time for a **DNR** Order-**Do Not Resuscitate!**

Is your "that" living on life support?

Place a DNR on your issue.

Flora Samuel

Out of my need for things to be different, the birth of this revelation was born. My desire was so overwhelming to teach the Word of God. I wanted others to be as happy as I was and just filled with joy, so immersed in the presence of the Lord.

During the year 2004 so many changes happened in my life; a relationship ended, I moved to a new place to live and I got a new job. Old things, useless things and unfruitful things were removed and I have to believe it was the will of God. Then other things began to happen. I began to have the urge to work out in the gym, so I committed myself to doing just that. I decided I was going to lose some weight. I began to modify my diet. Chicken became my main entrée; I cut out of my diet rice and bread. I began to drink nothing but diet drinks, which I always thought I would never do.

At this time I also began to embark on an even greater journey with the Lord. I started by trying to understand myself more and to try to understand why my relationship with a man of God ended, but the journey led me on a path that has not ended yet and I don't think that it will. I believe the Holy Spirit will continue to develop me and reveal the Lord to me in even greater ways, ways that are beyond explanation.

I began to fall in love all over again with the Lord. This time it was more, if you will allow me to use that word; the Lord began to wrap me in His presence in unbelievable ways. There were days after a while of studying His Word, looking up and researching scriptures that I became like a person walking on clouds. The revelation of Christ continued. Then the most incredible thing happened; the Lord opened up the windows of heaven and began to pour me out a blessing that I did not have room enough to store. He began to make real to me what love and forgiveness were all about. He unleashed His loving power upon me and in me, showing me what it means to love someone and to forgive someone. He revealed to me the awesome power of both. That I must say was the ultimate.

I then met a young woman at work; her vessel was filled with the power and love of God. Her mannerism (character) spoke so eloquently for her; she did not need to say a word. Her spirit was quite, meek and she was totally humble. This renewed a much needed renewal and faith in the people of God. That God still had some whom He personally had placed His mark upon. She wore her vessel as a shining beacon light as though she had arrived from heaven itself. I praise God for her.

My life continued on at this point with a few jabs from the enemy here and there. My heart still ached for the human love I had always seemed to hunger for my entire life. My dear sister always encouraged me to remember that my Heavenly Father knows the things I have need of and my desires. She reminded me to just pray about it. Her reasoning and sound advise I'm sure pleased the Lord.

After a while I learned that just wishing and hoping for things to be good, great and different were not enough. So I began to put action to my dreams and it seemed nothing still was working out. That made me even more discouraged, worse than before. Because this time I had tried and things still did not seem to work out for me the way I thought they would or should, or the way I simply would have liked them to. It was stand or doubt, will I still stand for the Lord, will I go on with the Lord, or will I turn back? Or choose to know that the Lord was allowing that time and that season. I was to know that He was in control, after all, He had said in His Word and probably a zillion times to me also that He would never leave me or forsake me; but because of all the bad breaks and the ones I didn't get, which I thought I should have; they were serving up doubt to me on huge plates; I became doubtful.

This taught me the difference between walking by faith and walking by sight. By sight, I looked at, viewed and then came to the conclusion that people were better than me because they never seem to experience the same missed breaks that I always seem to have experienced and that was not walking by faith.

I became almost cynical and I did to a degree (to cover the real truth-the real hurt and pain). I would be cynical at times because I was afraid to allow myself to feel. I knew I would become disappointed and discouraged again, I knew that spirit all too well, after all, it had been a constant companion, I always had to fight the feeling (spirit) of discouragement.

Had God planned for this life-long struggle? Was mankind, was I suppose to experience this struggle forever? Life forced me to walk by faith because there was nothing I could see in the natural that things were going to work out for me.
No one knew how close I was to committing suicide; things that I was experiencing in the natural were overwhelming and they were pushing me there. I found out that I was over-identifying with what I didn't get and what didn't happen that I thought should have for me, I had not reached a place in my life like in the scripture that says; Beloved, think it not strange concerning the fiery trials which is to try you, as though some strange thing happened to you. It has happen to mankind, to humanity; but you know the devil, he deceives you into thinking that it is just you that it is happening to and he adds to it saying you did something wrong, or there is something you didn't do. I believed him for years; but no more, not for this trial at least. I didn't know how to simply acknowledge it and recognize that it is the norm of life and at large the population experiences it, that these things were humanity experiences not just Flora's.

At times even when watching pastors and leaders on Christian Television, Satan used that against my mind. He was telling me how I ought to be also, like them and if I was not there, I was not doing something right. Something was wrong with me, so after hearing those words, those lies I came under condemnation, feeling inadequate; that I didn't measure up. (Remember this was a demon spirit I had dealt with for years). Comparing myself was mental torture; it robbed me of peace and was deadly. They were not the standard for my life; the Word of God was and is for my life the standard that I am to conform to. Amen.

CHAINS BROKEN

Just at a time when I thought finally, finally I'm here. I think I have reached the place of maturity, ready to go out in the things of the Lord. I moved from just dreaming and wishing to put action to my confession of faith. I thought surely it is now and then bam, nothing happens, except seemed like more obstacles, closed doors, nadda…

I then became disillusioned at this point, perplexed, I did not understand this new phase and place. After all, at this time, weren't the doors supposed to open and swing wide; now that I have gone through all these tests and trials, done all this work, devoted myself to learn more of God and His Christ's character. I allowed myself to be worked, disciplined and tutored by the Lord's hand and work in my life. Surely now it was time to go into all the world and share all the things He had placed in my heart and my soul, it was a part of me, I became it, the visions He had given me early on when I was innocent. So they were not vain thoughts and visions.

Then I started looking at my age and comparing it to the time I think I have left to fulfill God's will, and it seemed my life fell way short. That put fear in me, what if I don't live long enough to do what God called me to do. I started looking at it from this perspective and it seems hopeless and doomed. Match that with all the Christian television voices, 2007 this, 2007 that, that you should be doing this and you should be doing that, and so on and so on.

This created the most anxious and frustrating time again in my life. I found myself back to square one, where do I go from there? So I applied for a new job, (an Ishmael) couldn't wait on God, so let's go into works right, our own ideas. So this job was an ideal one, not to mention the pay increase that would come along with it. Well guess what? I didn't get the job and to make matters worse, I had a job that I hated and could wait to leave it, so all this sent me reeling back to why, why me, why can't I catch a break. This God thing, is it all that it is cracked up to be?

It seemed like every time something went wrong or didn't work out the way I thought it should, I blamed God, not Satan, after all, the promises I knew and had come to expect came from God and not Satan. Forgive me Lord, I know your plans for me have not changed, why must I be doubtful of that? But it was my expectations of stuff and not more of You. I was under the impression, the illusion that if I serve You that You would make things happen for me, so why were You not making them happen. My mind and my emotions raced backwards and forth from one extreme to the other, faith one day to all out doubt the next day; then finally settle in to faith, faith would win out. Thank God for Jesus, amen.

The torment of waiting was oh so surreal, but I learned that the wait was an asset and not a liability. I had to put it all behind me and go forth in the things of God. The tricks of the enemy of my soul was that it (whatever I did) would never be enough, but it was, after all, it was not what I did, it was what I believed, and that was the battle. I would move and fix myself in fear. Fear was the motivator; I would think if I just fixed myself and keep myself fixed, I would be ok. What is being ok, these things only took me into works. It counter-acted my faith, my trust in my God and Father. It was He who had begun the good work anyway, not me, so it was He who would and was going to complete it.

I would change my hair so many times until now today, my hair follicles are scorched and burnt. I have difficulty trying to get my hair to grow back in certain places and the thickness of it seems not to happen anymore. I couldn't seem to control anything else so I would work on my hair. A faulty mindset was in operation, I didn't let myself rest, I had to keep fixing myself, it was my weapon of defense as well as the issue at the same time, it was an obvious cycle that I couldn't control. I could never quit because if I stopped I would be consumed by this invisible force, this evil enemy; at least that is what I thought. The mind battle, the internal war....

Now, I know that I'm not a project to be worked on until I become perfect; the standard would forever be changing anyway (because it was based on false belief and evidence-all external), so it was like a pit without a bottom in it, so no matter how much you try to fill it, you will never be able to.

Battle in the mind, when I saw one person, I liked the way they looked, so I would mimic that person, then I would see another person and I would want to look like them, from blonde hair to red hair, whatever the case was, I would try it. See I turned myself into my own project; I had made myself into an idol. This went against God's grace for my life.

The last and the hardest thing for me to give up was "ME". I give up Lord my rights and the perfecting of myself to You. I repent and thank You for forgiving me.

I gave up working on myself; I gave myself to the renewing of my mind by the Word of God. I received God's grace for living a whole life; I resigned from working on myself as a project, an idol I had become to myself. Then I realize that there was nothing wrong, God loved me ever so much. He never said that I would not ever be afraid, He just told me to be of good courage for He had "already" overcome the world, the flesh and the devil. So here I am; I know that I will end up in victory. They were real things at the time, every man and woman of God have experienced these things, so why was I beating myself up? The answer is lack of faith, it is always the answer, I had been allowing the enemy to feed my thoughts, but my God, He is sovereign and He **REIGNS** and He intervened; thank You Lord.

But all of this gave me the compassion that is needed for a frail and faltering world and people; an imperfect humanity. The gift of compassion and mercy, just loving them, letting them know that Jesus loves them and that He heals hurt and wounded souls. These trials had been used also to remove all elements of judgment of others, because I would be reminded of where I had come from on my own journey.

In the end God began again to mightily increase the speed and the amount of revelation He was giving me. It seemed my spiritual vision and understanding increased in leaps and bounds. I began to be consumed with Him; I began to be God conscious like never before, it was as though He spread Himself increasingly wide in me. He began to fill me completely. He began to spill over into every area of my life; nothing went untouched by Him and His presence. My thought processes were all God-filled, God natured, it seemed as if other things began to fade away.

I'm consumed of God, this is the fulfillment of the yearning I had for so many years. Now I am whole and complete in Him, who I was positional all along, but now I know it …. Amen. Chains were broken off my mind and the way I thought.

VICTORY IN JESUS

I now teach the Word of God by revelation given me by the Holy Spirit. This is my story…. The Lord loves me so that He allowed me a test that was incredibly painful, but if that was what it took to completely set me free of all the bondages, then Your will Lord be done and it was. In order to be in ministry and be able to do it without the fear of man, due to the insatiable need I had to be accepted, approved of, to feel worthy, to feel ok about myself, these trials and tests of great magnitude had to take place, so there would be no denying of the Almighty power of the one and only True and Living God, Jesus Christ His Son, with the unmistakable use and power of His Holy and Wonderful Spirit. As Jesus said I must needs go through Samaria, some things are just plain ole necessary. Amen

The tests and trials were to break every mindset contrary to the will of God in my life and to crush every dependence upon man. The tests taught me so many things, yet they taught me everything. I am now completely free, like the Apostle Paul, I know how to be abased and abound, but always abounding in faith, no matter what the situation; I've learned not to be self-absorbed, no more making of myself an idol.

Flora Samuel

CHAINS BROKEN

Even while continuing my journey of deliverance; growing in grace, there were still dry dessert places that occurred from time to time and they were those places where I was not sure and not certain of the path to take, but one thing I do now and that is, I now accept every test, every trial and every lesson to be learned in a loving way, the fate of the Lord's hand for my life.

They are the sufferings and the joys of being Yours Lord. I no longer fight, doubt, accuse or question You my Lord. I realize it was Your love for me that You allowed all such to take place. How else would I know of Your all consuming love and thoughts of me, the wonderful plan You had for me, even before my birth. That I had been pre-ordained for this, it would be the working out of Your mighty love and strength that I would come to know. I would come to know that You are a Deliverer, so that I could lead Your people out of bondage, with the same love and compassion You had for me. Thank You Lord for staying with me till all my bitter trials became sweet, because of You. Yes, it was love in expression…..Love in action…. Amen

Freedom that was found in Christ Jesus, from discouragement to triumph…..

My mess, my pains, my every trial, every battle, hurt, disappointment and all the discouragement had purpose, it was there, but I couldn't see it or recognize it because I was overwhelmed by the situations and circumstances of life that was happening at the time. It is ironic that your mind does a default to the setting that tells you that you can't and that you won't. Then it reminds you of instances when you perceived in the past on things that didn't work out for you.

Before I close I want to talk about your "DEFAULT" Settings, like a computer, our mind has default settings, they are words spoken, life lived, perceived negatives, an up-bringing that was conditioned to failure, even though you were created to win. Again, isn't it ironic how your mind (naturally) and automatically go on auto-pilot to take over when you say you want to do something big, something significant in God or even in your natural life. When you say or want to change the direction of your life, get free from something, your mind defaults to, automatically tell you, say to you that you can't and usually it is telling you that you are not adequate enough, you don't have what it takes, it reminds you of your "perceived" shortcomings, remember, the place of origin where the inadequate, inaccurate "perceptions" are coming from. They originate from a place that was satanically influenced by Satan, the enemy of your soul. Amen. These erroneous thoughts are also part of the un-renewed mind, which is yet to receive and comprehend the will of God for your life. These "default" thoughts by default settings, also whisper the secret things you haven't told anyone, because you fear that they won't understand. You are ashamed of them. Satan has power in things we hold secret; things that we think and perceive as "wrong" or ungodly about ourselves; things that we did, so we don't open up and receive God's grace for those areas in our lives.

This auto-default setting of our minds always whisper, you don't have this and you don't have that, the very thing you think you need to complete the thing you desire. It is your mind your automatic default mindset, called your sub-conscious mind, which is usually critical in nature, because it has not been re-set by the Word of God like your conscious mind has, the top-level of your thinking.

There are two levels in which we must become "RENEWED" in, our conscious and sub-conscious. It is a proven fact that 97% of our day to day activities, thoughts and action are done by our subconscious, by habit not our conscious and only 3% of what we do on a day-to-day basis is done by our conscious mind. Wow, this is incredible, we think we are in control of our lives and that we are submitted to the Holy Spirit when we are not actually....

Two-Levels of thinking, our mindsets, controlled by a default. This is why the battle for overcoming which we are promised by God in His Word by Christ Jesus seems to elude us. The subconscious state of mind is in action to always cause you to revert back, come back to your "comfort" zone when you have decided to step out in faith and move forward in the things of God for your life.

We succumb to the 2nd level of thinking when we meet a challenge when moving forward in God. We must re-configure, re-compute and download the Word of God to our deepest level of thinking, the subconscious level. That is why the battle has been forever, it seems impossible to cross over to unshakeable faith in God; because all along our second level of thinking was under-minding our efforts, making us subject to its way of thinking.

It made us always think "LIMITATIONS", causing us to live out of the "MINUS" from the old nature, instead of the "PLUS" in God through Christ Jesus, the new nature. Every time we desire, I desired to do something "extraordinary", which should be the "norm" for the believer, my default setting of my thinking would say the reasons I couldn't and wouldn't be able to do it. The subconscious image of lack and not enough is now destroyed in the name of Jesus; it has been replaced with abundance in Jesus' name... Amen

I now soar, you soar, above in Christ Jesus in our mindset, the very places we once crawled, we soar, hallelujah......Amen, Amen....
Because God, my Father, our Father, my and your Savior Jesus Christ and His magnificent Holy Spirit have illuminated me and you and given us light where we once walked in darkness....

I am now to tell the world about Jesus Christ and His victory over Satan, that He has given unto us as Believers that same victory..... And by faith we receive it ....In Jesus' name.

I am convinced, persuaded as the Word says in my own mind and spirit, that the compulsions, the need I thought I had to have fulfilled by ungodly means, which kept an entry way, a door for my life to be accessed by Satan by what seems like my entire adult life through my emotions have now been shut, for good and forever…Amen.

When I tried to move forward and become free, it was the default thinking that having my passions and needs fulfilled was all that I consisted of and that was all I was. That was a horrible default setting. The Lord by His wonderful Holy Spirit revealed to me I am so much more than my emotions and having them fulfilled. There is more to life than emotions and for women this is a critical area that must be renewed at all cost. Why had it been so important for me to have my emotions fulfilled? It was what I knew; I had learned from childhood what I was living and I thought that was all I was. I didn't know life outside of my feelings and emotions; that the real life was what God had died to give me; it was my birth right in Christ Jesus.

The real life, now I take courage, I take courage Lord with You Holy Spirit, to live the un-limitless life, I no longer fear to live, to live the "TRUTH", I now dare to dream and vision the Almighty completed work on my behalf, that now I have to only receive it….. Amen in Jesus' name.

My mind now expands, praise be to God, this is what faith is all about. Revelation of the fact that I was from the beginning empowered to live this wonderful un-limitless life, the power of Christ in the life of the believer and the knowledge of knowing that we have power and authority over the works of the enemy and the un-renewed mind.

The expansion of Your glory being lived out through me Lord, the hugeness of Your Majesty; I have a new King and His name is Jesus.

Knowing what my rights are, who I am in Christ Jesus. Because I seek His righteousness first, His Kingdom and the way He has set forth everything in Jesus' name, I have the right to wholeness mentally and emotionally. Knowing these rights enable me to decree and proclaim what is rightfully mine.

CHAINS BROKEN

I am free, never to be bound again……

The conclusion of the old mind, I thought I had nothing else to offer, nothing else to give. There had been nothing else I could give, 95% of my life had been emotions and along with that came an equal compulsion to have them fulfilled; so I was consumed with having them fulfilled. I drove my partners and others crazy with trying to make them responsible for my every moment of happiness and guess what for every moment I was unhappy. I had failed to realize as I said in earlier dialogue that I was more than my feelings and my emotions. The learned attitude and accompanying behavior had rode with me from childhood.

The only way I could receive attention was by creating an emotional rage or outcry, create an emotional need, a helpless-poor me emotion and this would give me significance. I need my emotions fixed; can I have a fix? (From man). I needed a fix like compared to a junkie needing his next fix, his next high.

All of us have some drug of choice, mine wasn't a needle of heroin or a piece of crack either, but it was a man and the need of a resistant fight from him to make me feel better, significant, even though I said I wanted fulfillment, I also wanted that resistance, that gave me significance also. I really wanted them to resist my manipulation. (Ladies you know what I'm talking about) right…..

I became what I was being, a servant to my emotions and feelings. I should have never been a servant to them; they were to be my servants and to be use godly, by the use of the Holy Spirit. They were to be under my control, while I was under the control of the Holy Spirit. This all happened because I had unhealthy ideas, emotions and feelings from a faulty mindset, they were distorted views, irrationally formed by the life I had lived. This all kept an entry way for Satan to access my soulish realm, my mind and my emotions.

Periodically, as I said in previous chapters a certain amount of freedom would come, but the invisible enemy of the sub-conscious state of mind would pull me right back. But my message to you ends with sharing the previous chapter of the triumph reached in mind, soul and emotions.

We no longer have to live the life and lie of defeat, under the influence of Satan and the un-renewed two levels of thinking. Now for me the thought of whether or not I am accepted by someone does not determine for me my value or my worth. A person's actions or lack of them, neither determines my value or worth. These were extremely hard lessons to learn and I learned them at my own expense; failing to know my own value, I was mishandled, misused and abused; but no more!!!!. I live as one who is set free.

God created me uniquely and purposefully……

I am free, never to be bound again, Amen, Amen….. It is so, in Jesus' name……

All Of Us

We've learned that we are responsible for own happiness, no other person, material possession or external condition can make us happy or unhappy, we have learned to consciously and subconsciously choose thoughts that support our positive esteem and self confidence from a renewed mind by God's Word. Our lives have become joyful, peaceful and fulfilled.

Scripture focus: Philippians 4:8, (Paraphrased) finally, let us fix our minds and our thoughts on this; what is true, honorable, right, pure, lovely and admirable think on these things.

Flora Samuel

CHAINS HAVE BEEN BROKEN AND DESTROYED BECAUSE OF THE ANOINTING

THE POWER OF GOD'S WORD AND BY HIS SPIRIT

AND NOW

WE DECREE

OUR MINDS ARE FREE

OUR EMOTIONS ARE HEALTHY

AND

WE LIVE BY FAITH

CHAINS BROKEN

Scriptures to rely upon

I returned and saw under the sun, that the race is not to the swift nor the battle to the strong, neither yet bread to the wise, nor yet riches to men of understanding, nor yet favour to men of skill' but time and chance happeneth to them all. Ecclesiastes 9:11/KJV

I praise You because I am fearfully and wonderfully made; Your works are wonderful, I know that full well. Psalms 139:14/NIV

For I know My thoughts that I think toward you, saith the Lord, thoughts of peace and not of evil, to give you an expected end. Jeremiah 29:11/KJV

And be not conformed to this world; but be ye transformed by the renewing of your mind. Romans 12:2A/KJV

You (God) will keep in perfect peace him (you & I) whose mind is stayed on Thee, because he (We) trusteth in Thee. Isaiah 26:3/KJV/NIV

And the peace of God which passeth all understanding, shall keep your hearts and minds through Christ Jesus. Philippians 4:7/KJV

Therefore if any man be in Christ, he is a new creature; old things (damaged mindsets) are passed away; behold, all things are become new. II Corinthians 5:17/KJV

And **you** shall know the "Truth" and the "Truth" shall make **you** free. John 8:32/KJV

If the Son (Jesus Christ) shall make **you** free, **ye** shall be free indeed. John 8:36/KJV

There is a little bit of ground work to be laid, a foundation; so let's take a moment to do it.

Do you know Him, Jesus Christ as Savior and Lord?

I am extending to you an invitation to the best life ever.

A life with Christ

If you haven't given your life to Jesus Christ, would you with me take a moment to invite Him into your life? I promise you that your life will never be the same again.

First Time

(Say Aloud) Jesus I believe You are the Son of God and that You died and was raised from the dead. You took my place for the forgiveness of my sin. I ask you to come into my life, my heart and be my Savior and Lord.

See Scripture: Romans 10:9 &10 (Remember, this can be said your personal way, as long as you believe in your heart that what you are saying is "True" and "Truth".... Amen

For all those who have already accepted Him as your Savior and He is now your Lord, would you take a moment to renew your commitment to Him? Bind your heart afresh to His again..Amen

To all first time receivers of the new life in Christ, call a friend or someone and tell them about the most important decision you've ever made in your life. Then find a Word of God believing church home and get baptized-fully submerged in water.

If you need help finding a new church home or have questions about the decision you've just made, contact us. (Please see the contact information at the back of the book).

Flora Samuel

I have a saying that I remind myself of:

I can't be made wrong because I am right in my own sight.

I am complete in Christ Jesus, the fullness of the Godhead dwells in me fully……

God the Father, God the Son, and God the Holy Spirit.

I refuse to live confined to the dictates, viewpoints and boundaries of others and the traditions of men instead of the Word of God.

CHAINS BROKEN

If I may borrow a thought from a print out I obtained years ago, but it holds an incredible truth and I will add to it: At the end of the day all is a lie, if it is contrary to the Word of God…..

"It is between the clear Word of God and anything that conflicts with it".

SPEAK THESE SPIRITUAL BLESSINGS OVER YOU, BECAUSE THEY ARE GIVEN TO YOU OF YOUR HEAVENLY FATHER. AMEN

I AM BLAMELESS

I AM BLESSED

I HAVE FAVOR

I HAVE REST

I'M HOLY

I HAVE HOPE

I AM LOVED

I'M SANCTIFIED

I HAVE PEACE

I AM FAULTLESS

I HAVE JOY

I HAVE GRACE

I HAVE ABUNDANCE

I HAVE FREEDOM

I HAVE POWER

I HAVE NEW LIFE

I HAVE WISDOM

I AM FORGIVEN

CHAINS BROKEN

I AM AN HEIR OF GOD AND A JOINT-HEIR WITH JESUS CHRIST.... OF THE KINGDOM OF GOD AND ALL THAT IT ENTAILS………

Flora Samuel

Evidence of the changed life, from a witnessing pastor

JOURNEYCHURCH- MIRAMAR (GCI)

Following Christ and Making Disciples

We would like to take this opportunity to share a little about Sister Flora. She has been attending Journey Church for several months. When we first met her, we sensed a love for God and for the spiritual welfare for people, not just people in a congregation but for the body of Christ and those whose eyes have not yet been opened to God's incredible grace and love for them. Sister Flora lovingly ministers to all who come to her, others she is drawn to it seems by the Holy Spirit and God's love to help those grow in the relationship with Him. Her commitment to prayer in the Spirit, and her desire to listen to the Spirit of God is inspiring and uplifting. She has a spirit of joy and freedom in Christ that instead of pointing people to her lifts up Jesus Christ that all might be drawn unto Him. The Holy Spirit lay on Sister Flora's heart to share certain things with me and my wife, we were led to listen and hear what she felt the spirit was sharing with us through her. Not only were her words well received but ministered to us in love, power, and humility. Her humility and desire to point to Christ and not herself is not only refreshing, but brings great joy as we serve in the body together. Sister Flora belongs to the body of Christ, we praise God that she fellowships with us, but halleluiah! Sister Flora has seen the reality that there is only one church-God's church- one body, one faith, and one baptism, many rooms but one church. Recently on our praise, worship, and testimonial day, I was led by the spirit to ask Sister Flora to share a prayer and a few words of encouragement, she readily accepted and we were all blessed as she prayed and shared her joy, peace, and freedom in the Spirit. It is a blessing getting to know Sister Flora and we praise God that at this time the Lord has led her to fellowship at Journey Church as we all grow in the grace and knowledge of our Lord and savior Jesus Christ. We support her as the Spirit leads and believe that she is a tremendous blessing to all she comes into contact with. Please feel free to call me or if there is ever anything we can do to serve you all please let us know. May the God of salvation and grace shower His abundant blessings through His Spirit on you, your family, and ministry.

Sincerely

Charles Taylor

Senior Pastor

Journey Church-Miramar (GCI)

Flora Samuel

A response from my foundation pastor, Janna Hogan, Melbourne, Florida

Testimony of God's goodness and His mercy

From:
"Pastor Janna" <pastorjanna@jitk.org>

Beloved of the Lord,
How blessed I was to have received word from you....

Your kind words met my heart at a time of need....bless you for such exhortation and encouragement......

We are all well.....the ministry team and the few at JITK
We are extremely active in the Spirit of the Lord and doing our annual outreaches with huge successes......
yet.....our local church remains very small.....

Over the years.....the Lord has entrusted to us many souls.....
We're His servants and grateful to be......and remain in faith for all He has for us......

I believe I told you that we're on the web and do web cast the services. LIVE at service times and run available archived 24/7
www.jitk.org

I am most grateful to the Lord for using me as you said, to birth in you what He desired.....and yes.....many others....

He has continued to do that.....with specific individuals He's marked for special services....
I'm honored and humble to be part of His plan for you and them.....

Beautiful Flora.....a flower destined to flourish in the garden of God.....in the scared soil of His Word.....there His seed in you develops you.....and through you.....to make manifest a testimony of the Lord.....a sweet aroma............a healing therapy for others.....from heaven....
Be blessed.......continue to bloom for Him........

With Love beyond the flesh.........Pastor Janna.

CHAINS BROKEN

This book was written on being delivered from mindsets that binds and hinders; mindsets that keeps us from being all that we can be in Christ and because of my own struggle to find freedom in Christ. Mindsets that keep us locked into non-producing and non-productive cycles; sometimes even destructive behaviors. These mindsets do not allow you to expand, don't allow you to become expansive, positive, glory-filled-faith-filled people of God.

These mindsets keep us locked into repetitive actions and drama, unsuccessful, whether it's spiritual or naturally. We can't seem to go forward, our minds causes us to even live in fear of the productive-faith-filled life, of the fruit-producing life of Christ; bountifully excelling in the things of God.

But there is HOPE.....

His name is Jesus, the Christ, the Anointed One, and the One that is waiting and wanting to destroy that yoke, every yoke of bondage over our lives, whatever it may be. Amen

I pray this prayer for you and me that the God of all grace will strengthen and settled us after we have been tried for a while.

That we may be delivered, set-free and healed in the spirit of our minds and our soul in Jesus' name.

That Christ may dwell in our hearts by faith; that you and I being rooted and grounded in love, may be able to comprehend/understand with all the saints what is the breath, length, depth and height and to know the love of Christ which passeth knowledge that we be filled with all the fullness of God.

Flora Samuel

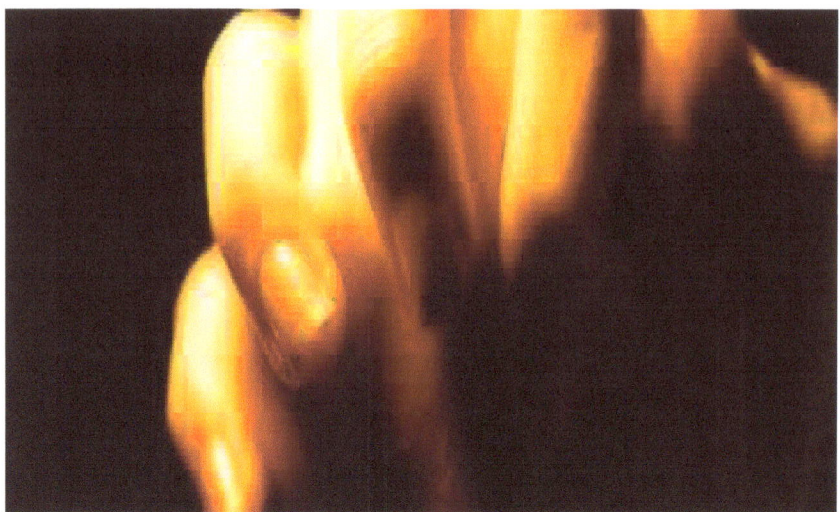

I pray we would be strengthen with might by His Spirit (that is we be divinely enabled to live the Christian life) in our inner man.

That you and I be able to comprehend/understand the "LOVE" (all that it entails) of Christ, that to be better able to understand the enormous love Christ has for us.

That you and I might be filled with all the fullness of God (His life, character and His virtues) God Himself (Christ) be fully developed in us.

So let's receive His grace-the ability to come out from under and move up and over to the top in Him, in Jesus' name. Amen

Now unto Him that is able to do exceeding, abundantly above all that we may ask or think, according to the power that worketh in us, unto Him be glory in the church by Christ Jesus throughout all ages, world without end….Amen and Amen….

CHAINS BROKEN

JESUS SAID, "COME UNTO ME ALL OF YOU WHO ARE WEARY AND CARRY HEAVY BURDENS AND I WILL GIVE YOU REST". MATTHEW 11:28/NLT

A testimony of God's grace from the first ex-husband of this book.

What the enemy meant for evil, God turned it around for His glory...

Journey

Tribute to my one and only true love, Flo.

You are an inspiration in my life's journey you molded and shaped me when I was entangled in the devil's nest. Little did I know that we would be divorced twice but now we are engaged in our lordship's Service. From Gainesville through Melbourne, Orlando. Iceland, Norway, Sweden and finally Denmark we both took the journey. I will never forsake nor leave you Flo, and one day we will reunite in heavenly love everlastingly. What a journey. Love you Flo and thanks for sharing your life with me.

CHAINS BROKEN

My Beloved, He is mine and I am His...

Flora Samuel

Remember,

Jesus:
the fulness of
the Godhead,
bodily

–Colossians 2:9

Dwells in you and me… Amen…

Flora Samuel

To contact the author write:

Flora Samuel Ministries

6720 Arbor Drive # 106

Miramar, Florida 33023

Or call: (954) 240-3845

Internet Website: florasamuelministries.com

Email Address: florasamuel2012@yahoo.com

Please email your testimony of help received from this book. **Your prayer requests are welcome.**

About the Author

Flora is a passionate follower of Jesus Christ and is a licensed and ordained Apostle and Minister of the Gospel of Jesus Christ. Her passion is to see the Body of Christ set free and living the abundant life of God; to help those that are mentally and emotionally bound. "The most powerful force behind my determination and passion is my own liberation from a once previous and most oppressed mindset; now I desire to share and impart this liberation to others".

www.ingramcontent.com/pod-product-compliance
Lightning Source LLC
Chambersburg PA
CBHW042309150426
43198CB00001B/16